CW01509984

SHORT STORIES

ENGLISH
FLUENCY PRACTICE SERIES

INTERMEDIATE LEVEL

VOLUME 4

by Alexander Pavlenko
CREATE SPACE EDITION

PUBLISHED BY:

Sapcrystals plc on CreateSpace

SHORT STORIES

INTERMEDIATE LEVEL

ISBN-13: 978-1511837286

ISBN-10: 1511837284

FOREWORD

Based on the Speech Plasma Method, the book is designed to teach students to speak English at intermediate level. The volume contains twenty short stories and special training drills. This volume will enable foreign students of English to feel more comfortable with the language at a more advanced level. The book is a collection of stories told by people in everyday conversational manner. The stories are accounts of incidents or ideas which the people interviewed consider interesting or entertaining. They are not intended as great works of literature, rather as examples of people using their language naturally. The stories are the sort of tales that you might hear in a pub or at a party, reflections on anything from weather and inquisitive neighbours to a passion for music and how it can help handicapped children. At times amusing, surprising, entertaining or simply hard to believe, they are all related in the kind of natural informal style which language learners so often wish to imitate. This collection will help show you how to do just that. Audiobook version of the volume is available in the Kindle Store.

CONTENTS

A Trip to Crete

Last year my wife and I spent our holidays in Crete, the southernmost island in Greece, and we made lots of little excursions there into the countryside. On one occasion, we wanted to visit the south side of the island, where there are some ruins from the Roman times and from a former monastery. We went there by bus, travelling along tiny little windy roads. It was quite frightening to watch how the bus driver was manoeuvring the vehicle around all of the twisty curves in the road, quite breathtaking. At every curve we were scared that the bus would crash, and the bus driver had to signal with his horn at each turning as it was impossible to see if any traffic was coming from the other direction and there wasn't enough space on the road for two vehicles to pass side by side.

When we arrived at the nearest bus stop to the ruins, we could see them in the distance, and we could see that there were only two ways to get there - on foot, or by boat, if we had one, which we didn't. So we started walking in that direction, along a dried up river bed. From the map it seemed that the distance we had to walk was about three kilometres, but it must have been longer, as it took us about three hours of difficult climbing and scrambling over rocks to get there.

At one point on the way we reached the top of a hill, from which we had an amazing view of the ruins. There we met a boy from France, who we shared friendly gestures with, but couldn't really speak with as we didn't speak a foreign language. We climbed down from there together, into the grounds of the ruins. There was a fence blocking our path, but it was quite small and easy to climb over.

In the grounds of the ruins were some very twisty, gnarled old olive trees, and at the entrance we found a beautiful mosaic from the Roman times, leading to many little paths. The monastery was very small. Each of the monks' cells were just tiny little box-like rooms, two by three metres in size. The whole place had a beautiful, ancient atmosphere.

By the time we got there we were very tired after so much walking, and weren't looking forward to the long trek back to the bus stop. We weren't even sure that we would get there in time for the last bus. Fortunately, we met a fisherman on the beach, who was there fishing for octopuses. He was kind enough to take us back to the road by boat, which only took about ten or fifteen minutes, and the walk to the bus stop from where he dropped us off was very short. We were well in time to catch the bus. We were very happy, if a little exhausted, after a nice, interesting trip.

A Trip to Crete

1. Where did they spend their holidays last year?
2. What did they do while on holiday?
3. Why did they want to visit the south part of the island?
4. How did they get there?
5. Why did they find their trip frightening?
6. What were they afraid of?
7. Why did the driver have to signal with his horn at turnings?
8. How could they get to the ruins from the bus stop?
9. How long did it take them to get there?
10. Where did they meet a boy from France?
11. What was the trouble communicating with him?
12. What did they have to get over when they got to the ruins?
13. What did they find at the entrance of the ruins?
14. What size were the monks' cells?
15. What did they think of the place?
16. Why weren't they eager to walk back to the bus stop?

17. What could happen if they had walked to the bus stop?

18. Who did they meet?

19. What was the fisherman doing there?

20. What was the favour he did them?

21. How long did the boat trip take?

22. Did the fisherman drop them off at the bus stop?

23. How did they reach the bus stop then?

24. Did they catch the last bus?

25. How did they feel at the end of the day?

A Trip to Crete

Training 1

They went there by bus, travelling along tiny little windy roads. It was quite frightening to watch how the bus driver was manoeuvring the vehicle around all of the twisty curves in the road, quite breathtaking. At every curve they were scared that the bus would crash, and the bus driver had to signal with his horn at each turning as it was impossible to see if any traffic was coming from the other direction.

Training 2

There were only two ways to get to the ruins - on foot, or by boat. So they started walking in that direction, along a dried up river bed. From the map it seemed that the distance they had to walk was about three kilometres, but it must have been longer, as it took them about three hours of difficult climbing and scrambling over rocks to get there.

Training 3

At one point on the way they reached the top of a hill, from which they had an amazing view of the ruins. There they met a boy from France, who they shared friendly gestures with, but couldn't really speak with as they didn't speak a foreign language. They climbed down from there together, into the grounds of the ruins. There was a fence blocking their path, but it was quite small and easy to climb over.

Training 4

In the grounds of the ruins were some very twisty, gnarled old olive trees, and at the entrance they found a beautiful mosaic from the Roman times, leading to many little paths. The monastery was very small. Each of the monks' cells were just tiny little box-like rooms, two by three metres in size. The whole place had a beautiful, ancient atmosphere.

Training 5

Fortunately, they met a fisherman on the beach, who was there fishing for octopuses. He was kind enough to take them back to the road by boat, which only took about ten or fifteen minutes, and the walk to the bus stop from where he dropped them off was very short. They were well in time to catch the bus. They were very happy, if a little exhausted, after a nice, interesting trip.

Pub Music in Edinburgh

I first became involved in playing Irish music many years ago when I first visited Ireland, and was greatly inspired after attending some great folk festivals there. The first one I went to was in County Sligo, in Ballisadare. There were so many great groups playing there - DeDanaan, The Bothy Band, Clannad, all the best known Irish musicians of that time. There were thousands of tents and thousands of people everywhere, and there was a really great atmosphere. The whole thing lasted for three days, and I had a really nice time.

What struck me most was the power of the sound of the fiddle, such a fantastic instrument. I took up the fiddle when I was a small child, but dropped it when I came to the age of about thirteen. But after seeing those folk play in Ireland, well, I had to pick it up again. I brought some sheet music back from Ireland, and when I got back home to Dorchester, joined a local folk music club and tried a few tunes. First we played the tunes very slowly. You wouldn't recognize them because they were so slow, but gradually I learnt a few of them by heart.

Then I moved to Edinburgh, because my wife, Sophie, is a scientist, and she got a grant to go and work at the University of Edinburgh. She was looking for a place to work where she could work well and expand her knowledge, and at the same time somewhere where I would feel happy. We considered Ireland and Scotland, and eventually decided upon Scotland. I found some work there too. I am also a scientist, a biologist, specializing in mosses. There are so many mosses in Scotland, and I knew people up there who were also involved in studying mosses, so I found myself working for the peat land section of the Scottish Heritage Trust. At home I'd just finished a big study on heavy metal deposition, which can be gauged by analyzing mosses, and I had some good opportunities to talk with other experts about my results, as well as to collect mosses.

My time in Edinburgh was one of the finest times of my life, because I enjoyed my work, and there was great music in the evenings. I went out three times a week to folk music sessions, which took place in a few of the local pubs, and met some really great musicians there, some lovely people. We'd go in and sit down in the pub at the beginning of the evening, have a drink, and would be chatting away when someone would get out their instrument and start playing. Then others that knew the tune they were playing would join in. Some people would play regularly in each pub, and there were always people passing through. The first session I went to I discovered by luck. I just went into the pub and saw that there were people playing, and once you're in one session it's easy to find out from the musicians the times and places of others. I really was a bad fiddle player at the time, but I tried to play a bit and listened a lot, and people were very kind to me and took me to lots of sessions. I'm not a great player at the moment, but I think I've improved a bit since then! I took a portable tape recorder with me and recorded, session by session, many tunes, and tried to learn some of them when I had some spare time. I learned a lot from listening and watching how others played - and there were some really talented players in Edinburgh at that time, like John Martin, for example. You can't imagine how good some of the playing was. There were also people playing the mandolin and the flute, Irish pipes and guitars.

A lot of people from Northern Ireland, particularly from Donegal, used to come to the Edinburgh sessions, and they were a strong influence. There are some pubs where people play Irish music there, and some where people play Scottish music. There were always more people playing in the Irish sessions, maybe because Scottish music is usually played by a solo instrument, maybe with a guitar accompaniment, whereas in Irish music you often find five or six fiddles playing together, which is, I think, more exciting. Also, in the Scottish sessions, you'd very rarely hear any songs, which were more common in the Irish ones.

I wouldn't have liked to live in Edinburgh forever, but I had a really fantastic time there and I was sad to leave. The time there was too short, even for our kids. The kids went to school there, and for our son it was the first time he'd been to school. They both picked up a strong Scottish accent!

Pub Music in Edinburgh

1. When did Greg first become involved in playing Irish music? *Long time ago (when he visited Ireland*

2. What was the first festival he visited like? *Was amazing*

3. What struck him most at the festival? *ever lots of people / the sound*

4. When did he take up fiddle? *When he was little*

5. Why did he have to learn playing it again? *in Dorchester*

6. How did he pick up the fiddle back home? *joined a local*

7. Why did they move to Edinburgh? *wife job folk club*

8. What did Greg and his wife do? *scientist*

9. What about Greg's work in Scotland? *& mosses*

10. Why did he enjoy living in Edinburgh? *work and music*

11. How often did he go to folk music sessions? *3 x week*

12. Where did they take place? *fave local pub*

13. What did they do at the sessions? *play music and drink*

14. How did he happen to discover those sessions? *Luck*

15. How did he turn into a regular session player?

16. What kind of fiddle player was Greg at the time? *Very bad*

17. Has he improved since then? *Yes*

18. What did he do to improve? *lissent people*

19. What other instruments did some of the musicians play?

20. Did they only play Scottish music in the pubs in Edinburgh? *No Irish*

21. How did it happen that there were Irish sessions in Edinburgh? *Lots Irish people*

22. Why were there more people playing in the Irish sessions? *different music*

23. Were songs typical for Scottish sessions? ∧ instrumen

24. How did he feel when he had to leave Edinburgh? sad

25. Why was that time prominent for their children, too? yes

Pub Music in Edinburgh

Training 1

Greg first became involved in playing Irish music many years ago when he first visited Ireland. He was greatly inspired after attending some great folk festivals there. The first one he went to was in County Sligo. There were so many great groups playing there. There were thousands of tents and people everywhere, and there was a really great atmosphere.

Training 2

Greg took up the fiddle when he was a small child, but dropped it when he came to the age of about thirteen. But after seeing those folk play in Ireland, Greg had to pick it up again. He brought some sheet music back from Ireland, and when he got back home, joined a local folk music club and tried a few tunes. First they played the tunes very slowly. But gradually Greg learnt a few of them by heart.

Training 3

He moved to Edinburgh, because his wife got a grant to work at the University of Edinburgh. She was looking for a place to work where she could expand her knowledge, and at the same time somewhere where Greg would feel happy. They eventually decided upon Scotland. Greg found some work there too. He is a biologist, specialising in mosses. And he had some good opportunities to talk with other experts, as well as to collect mosses.

Training 4

While they were living in Edinburgh Greg went out three times a week to folk music sessions. They'd go in, sit down in the pub, and have a drink, and someone would get out their instrument and start

8

playing. Then others would join in. Greg really was a bad fiddle player at the time, but he learned a lot from listening and watching how others played.

Training 5

A lot of people from Northern Ireland used to come to the Edinburgh sessions, and they were a strong influence. There are some pubs where people play Irish music, and some where people play Scottish music. There were always more people playing in the Irish sessions, maybe because in Irish music you often find five or six fiddles playing together or because songs were more common in the Irish sessions.

Balalaikas in Syria

My friend Alexander, who is Russian, told me an interesting story about a trip he made to Damascus, in Syria, a few years ago. He was working in a city in the heart of Siberia as an interpreter for a dancing group, composed of boys and girls aged between about fourteen and seventeen. They were a very professional dancing group, as they'd all started dancing at about the age of six, and had been training intensively since then, every day, learning many different types of dances, so it was very impressive to see them. It was a real pleasure for my friend to work with them, and to see them dance so often. Every time he looked at them he couldn't help admiring them, as they danced so magnificently, better than many adult dancing groups that he'd seen.

Anyway, they travelled to Damascus in July or August, in the middle of summer, so it was rather hot in Siberia at that time, about twenty-nine degrees Celsius, so everybody was sweating. He said to them before they left, "Don't forget where we are going, we're going to Damascus, very close to the desert, and it's going to be something like forty-seven or even fifty degrees. "

When they arrived at the airport, however, and got out of the plane, they didn't believe that they were in a desert region, as they all felt a little bit chilly! When it was announced at the airport that it was just eighteen degrees, they couldn't believe their ears.

The next day, however, the heat wave came, and it was blistering hot. The temperature reached forty-seven degrees, and so during the day it was almost impossible for my friend and his group to go out into the street without staying in the shade. They could walk along covered walkways, or stay under the canvas awnings of cafes, but it was absolutely unbearable to be in the open.

My friend said that during the daytime in the summer there it is just like a dead city, with nearly empty streets with only very few people walking here and there and no other signs of life. But when the sun goes down, at about nine o'clock in the evening, life there really begins. All of the people come out into the streets, the cafes and restaurants open, and the social life starts. They go to parties, visit each other, buy and sell things, go to the cinemas - everything starts at nine in the evening and carries on until about two or three in the morning. For my friend it was like an upside-down world, as in Siberia everything closes at about nine, life finishes and everybody goes to bed.

Another thing that surprised Alex was that whereas in Russia it's very unusual for children to go out with their parents to restaurants and to places in the evening, in Damascus it's normal. The children may be three or four years old; you will be sitting and drinking and talking, and the children either sit down next to their parents or, more usually, run around between the tables and play. This was so unusual for my friend to experience, especially as Russia had been so restricted because of the Iron Curtain and he'd never had the opportunity to travel abroad before.

Their dancing tour was a great success. They were in several cities - Damascus, Aleppo and two or three more, and in each place that they danced the audiences went wild. They applauded and called for encores again and again and again. They were accompanied by a small group of musicians playing Russian instruments, balalaikas, and this was very unusual for the local people who were mostly Arabs, as their music was absolutely different, so they were altogether amused, amazed and thoroughly entertained.

They were especially successful in Aleppo, as thirty thousand Armenians live there. Armenia was a republic of the Soviet Union, and when they learnt that a group from Russia were playing, and also that they played music by Khachaturian, the famous Armenian composer, they flocked to the performance. They were fantastically well-received. The audience applauded and encored them many times and were very enthusiastic, maybe because they liked this music so much and felt a deep connection with it.

They stayed in a beautiful five-star hotel, with luxurious facilities, swimming pools, huge four-course meals, top-class service and things like this, and that was such a surprise for my friend, who had never been out of Russia before in his life. It was an absolutely fantastic experience for him, one of the greatest experiences of his life.

Balalaikas in Syria

1. Where did Alexander travel?
2. What was he doing then?
3. How did those teenagers become professionals so early?
4. When did they travel to Damascus?
5. What was the weather like in Siberia when they left?
6. What did Alexander warn his group about?
7. What surprised them when they arrived at the airport?
8. What was the temperature like the next day?
9. How could they get around in the city during the day?
10. What was Damascus like during the daytime?
11. When does life really begin?
12. What do the locals do in the evening?
13. Is such a vivid night life typical for Siberia?
14. What was another thing that surprised Alexander?
15. Had he travelled a lot before this trip?
16. How did the audience meet the group?
17. What was unusual for the local public in terms of music?
18. Where were they especially successful?
19. What could be the reason for that?
20. Whose music did they play among others?
21. How did the audience receive them in Aleppo?
22. Where did they stay?
23. What facilities were there at those hotels?

24. Why was it such a great surprise for Alexander?

25. What did he think of that trip?

Balalaikas in Syria

Training 1

My Russian friend Alexander made a trip to Syria some years ago. He was working in a city in the heart of Siberia as an interpreter for a dancing group, composed of boys and girls. They were a very professional dancing group, as they'd all started dancing at about the age of six, and had been training intensively since then. Every time he looked at them he couldn't help admiring them, as they danced better than many adult dancing groups that he'd seen.

Training 2

They travelled to Damascus in the middle of summer. When they arrived at the airport, however, it was announced that it was just eighteen degrees, so they couldn't believe their ears. The next day, however, the heat wave came, and it was blistering hot. The temperature reached forty-seven degrees, and so during the day it was absolutely unbearable to be in the open.

Training 3

During the daytime in the summer Damascus is just like a dead city, with nearly empty streets with only very few people and no other signs of life. But when the sun goes down life there really begins. All of the people come out into the streets, the restaurants open, they go to parties, visit each other, buy and sell things, go to the cinemas - everything starts at nine in the evening and carries on until about two or three in the morning.

Training 4

Their dancing tour was a great success. They were in several cities, and in each place that they danced the audiences went wild. They applauded and called for encores again and again. They were accompanied by a small group of musicians playing Russian instruments, balalaikas, and this was very unusual for the local people, as their music was absolutely different, so they were altogether amused, amazed and thoroughly entertained.

Training 5

They stayed in a beautiful five-star hotel, with luxurious facilities, swimming pools, huge four-course meals, top-class service and things like this, It was an absolutely fantastic experience. This was so unusual for my friend, especially as Russia had been so restricted because of the Iron Curtain and he'd never had the opportunity to travel abroad before.

Lost and Found

I'll tell you about the time I spent living in Norway. I had a girlfriend when I was there named Helga, and we used to go away sometimes to her family house, which was 2000 metres up in the mountains, and a very good base for skiing. We used to go up the mountains with a rucksack and skis on our backs, spend the day skiing, and then come back down and sit by the fire, and then Helga's Dad would beat me at chess: he'd just trap my king and I'd lose. . .

I was in Norway because I was working as an archaeologist, specializing in mediaeval archaeology, in the town of Trondheim, which is nowadays not that large, but was the capital of Norway in the Middle Ages, when Norway had a large empire, which included the Shetland and Orkney Isles, Ireland for a while, Iceland and Greenland. So it was a very rich town, and we dug it up, and there was a lot left from those times. We were not sure why there was a lot left, but a lot of old pots, and old leather and wooden articles survived. We found loads, especially things like forks and spoons, everyday objects.

We found a lot of rune-sticks, which was very exciting. What we were digging up was generally bits of wood, chips and chunks, and some of these lumps of wood had runes on them. Runes are a kind of writing which was used in Viking and mediaeval Norway. They are often thought to have been magical symbols, and in fact they may have also functioned in this way, but primarily they were used for simple writing, as they didn't have paper but had tons of wood. The symbols are made up of straight lines, because if you have a knife and a piece of wood, this is the easiest way to make letters. Obviously, you couldn't write books, or long texts, but it was a good system of conveying messages.

The content was often quite mundane, things like "Thorsson made me" or the alphabet, which is called the "Futhark" as the first letters were F-U-T-H-A-R-K. There was one strange one with something about Jerusalem written on it, which we couldn't work out. Some of them were just wrong, I mean what was written on them was gibberish, just letters that didn't really mean anything. These were all found in the rubbish, you see, and we think that there may have been people learning there, in kind of runic schools, where people had to write the alphabet twenty times and things like that.

We had buckets of water, and when we found something, a little piece of wood or something like that, we washed it and took a close look to see if there was anything there. Any runes we found were written down, and as it wasn't in modern Norwegian - the runes were written in mediaeval Norwegian- someone had to get a book out, first of all to find out what letters the runes represented and then to find out what the text meant.

We found a lot of objects that we couldn't identify. We found a very nice thing one day. Sonja, a Swedish woman who had been digging in the corner, suddenly said, "Whooah, look at this", and carried this thing towards me. From a distance it looked just like a little piece of wood, but when it was about a yard away I could see that it was a little king from a chess set. It was really, really exciting. To find the king was nice, not a pawn or a bishop, for example. We were really lucky that it came out in a lump, and we didn't scrape his head off, as we were cutting sections of earth to examine one section at a time, and Sonja had spotted his head sticking up out of the ground. I think somebody had cut off his nose by mistake, but the rest of him was intact. The find more than made up for my losing my own king so many times!

Lost and Found

1. Where did this story take place?
2. Where did Thomas and his girlfriend use to go sometimes?
3. What did they use to do there?
4. Who would usually win at chess in the evening?
5. What was he doing in Norway?

6. What did Trondheim use to be?

7. Why was it a good place for digging?

8. What did they find there?

9. What finds were especially exciting?

10. What are runes?

11. What were runes used for?

12. Why did the Vikings prefer wood to paper?

13. What are the runic symbols like?

14. What could be the reason for that?

15. What about the content of their finds?

16. How did they explain that some of the texts did not mean anything?

17. What did they need buckets of water for?

18. What language were runes written in?

19. How did they manage to find out what they meant?

20. Who found the most interesting find?

21. What did it look like from a distance?

22. What did it turn out to be?

23. What was lucky about this find?

24. Was it absolutely intact?

25. What did Thomas feel about this find?

Lost and Found

Training 1

Thomas spent some time living in Norway. He and his girlfriend Helga used to go away sometimes to her family house, which was 2000 metres up in the mountains. They used to go up the mountains with a rucksack and skis on their backs, spend the day

19

skiing, and then come back down, sit by the fire, and then Helga's Dad would beat Thomas at chess: he'd just trap his king and Thomas would lose.

Training 2

He was in Norway because he was working as an archaeologist in Trondheim. It was the capital of Norway in the Middle Ages, when Norway had a large empire, which included the Shetland and Orkney Isles, Ireland, Iceland and Greenland. So it was a very rich town. They dug it up, and there were a lot of old pots, and old leather and wooden articles left from those times.

Training 3

They found a lot of rune-sticks. Runes are a kind of writing which was used in Viking and mediaeval Norway. They are often thought to have been magical symbols, but primarily they were used for simple writing, as they didn't have paper but had tons of wood. The symbols are made up of straight lines. Obviously, you couldn't write books, but it was a good system of conveying messages.

Training 4

The content was often quite mundane or just the alphabet. Some of them were just wrong and gibberish, just letters that didn't really mean anything. These were all found in the rubbish, and they thought that there may have been people learning there, in kind of runic schools, where people had to write the alphabet twenty times and things like that.

Training 5

They found a very nice thing one day. It was a little king from a chess set. It was really, really exciting to find the king, not a pawn or a bishop, for example. They were really lucky that it came out in a lump, and they didn't scrape his head off. Somebody had cut off his nose by mistake, but the rest of him was intact. The find more than made up for Tomas's losing his own king so many times!

Holidays in Scotland

When I was a teenager, my pals and I went off camping in Arran, which is an island off the west coast of Scotland. We arrived by ferry at Brodick, and went off looking for a place to camp. We found a very nice place along the sea front to put up our tents, which was a peninsula, next to a golf course. We pitched our tents there, and spent some time beach-combing and playing football, if I remember well, and then when it got dark we decided to go to the local town for a drink. We decided to take a short cut across the golf course, and it was completely black, and none of us had a torch. We set off anyway, across this completely dark golf course, which we didn't know had some burns - ditches with little streams at the bottom - running across it. So we were marching along merrily towards the pub, when splish!, splash!, splosh!, we found ourselves knee-deep in water after falling into one of the streams. We dragged ourselves out and continued onwards to the pub.

The pub was nothing special, but we had a few drinks there, and when we finally got back, taking the road instead of returning across the golf course, we couldn't find the tents, or even the peninsula on which we'd camped. "What's going on? What's happened? Where are our tents?" we asked ourselves. It turned out that the area where we'd set up the tents wasn't really a peninsula at all, but that when the tide came in it became an island. So the tide had come in and cut us off from our tents. For the second time that evening we got wet feet, as to reach our tents we had to roll up our trousers, take off our shoes and socks and wade across to them.

At the time I was living in Elgin in the district of Moray, which is quite a nice area in the East of Scotland. It's famous for not having any thunderstorms. It has the fewest thunderstorms of anywhere in Britain, and is also well known for its whisky, as it is in the heart of the whisky distilling area, and has much fertile land for growing barley, and nearby there are hills where there is peat and fresh spring water, which you need to make whisky. So all of the famous whiskies come from there, like Glenfiddich and Glengrant, for example. There's a shop there where many of them are bottled, called Gordon Simpson's or something like that, and this shop sells about five hundred types of whisky, all from local producers. They have really special whiskies there, some thirty years old. In this shop we found a bottle which was produced at a distillery which I used to live next door to, called the Longmorne distillery, and even though we lived right next to this distillery we had never sampled its produce, so we bought a bottle. It was awful. It tasted like paint-stripper!

Another time I went camping was on the Isle of Iona. We camped in the north-west corner, I think. Iona is a very special island, which is historically important because Saint Columba lived there and founded a monastery there - he was the man who brought Christianity, in the form of the Celtic church, to Scotland, from Ireland. The story goes that he left on a very small boat from Ireland, and stopped on another island further south and wanted to settle there, but discovered that from this island they could still see Ireland, so they moved on to Iona, from which they couldn't see Ireland, so they wouldn't feel homesick.

It's a very beautiful island, with the monastery, a very nice mediaeval church, and beautiful, very ancient rocks, which, due to the movement of the geographical strata, consist of lovely, pretty, marble-type old rocks. There is a very special, unique, magical atmosphere there. The water surrounding the coast is very clear and blue, and there are some wonderful clean beaches there, with little rock-pools dotted about with little fish, crabs, and starfish in them, and lots of seaweed and driftwood scattered along the shore.

The weather is amazing, as it changes every fifteen or twenty minutes, so it can be pouring down with rain one minute, and then bright and sunny the next.

Anyway, we camped in the north-west corner where there is a farmer who lets you camp on his land, which is basically a strip of grass next to the beach. It's a lovely sandy beach with lots of driftwood, so we made a fire there and sat around it cooking soup in an old pot that he lent us and baking potatoes in the fire, drank a bottle of whisky, walked up and down collecting nicely shaped pieces of driftwood and watched the sun set on the horizon.

Holidays in Scotland

1. Where did Joey and his pals go off camping?
2. What was special about the place where they put up their tents?
3. How did they spend the day?
4. What were their plans for the evening?
5. Why did they decide to go across the golf course?
6. What did the course have?
7. What happened when they were marching across it?
8. Did they reach the pub after all?
9. Which way did they get back?
10. What did they see when they got back?
11. What did the area turn out to be?
12. What did they have to do to reach the tents?
13. What was that district famous for?
14. Why is the region so perfect for distilling whisky?
15. What did they buy in a specialised whisky shop?
16. What was it like?
17. What was another place he went camping in Scotland?
18. Why is the Isle of Iona so historically prominent?
19. Why did Saint Columba settle on it?
20. What can you find on the Isle of Iona?
21. What about the sea surrounding it?
22. What is really amazing about the weather there?

23. Where did they camp?

24. What was that part of beach like?

25. What did they do there?

Holidays in Scotland

Training 1

Joey and his pals went off camping in an island off the west coast of Scotland. They arrived by ferry. Then they found a nice place along the sea-front, which was a peninsula. When it got dark, they went to a pub. They took a short cut across the golf course, which had some little streams. So they were marching along, when they fell into one of the streams. They dragged themselves out and continued onwards to the pub.

Training 2

When they finally got back they couldn't find the tents, or even the peninsula on which they'd camped. It turned out that the area where they'd set up the tents wasn't really a peninsula at all, and when the tide came in it became an island. So the tide had cut them off from their tents. For the second time that evening they got wet feet, as they had to roll up their trousers, take off their shoes and socks and wade across to the tents.

Training 3

At the time he was living in Elgin in the district of Moray, which is in the heart of the whisky distilling area. It has much fertile land for growing barley, and nearby there are hills where there is peat and fresh spring water, which you need to make whisky. So all of the famous whiskies come from there, like Glenfiddich and Glengrant, for example.

Training 4

Another time Joey went camping was on the Isle of Iona. Saint Columba, who brought Christianity to Scotland, founded a monastery there. It's a very beautiful island, with the monastery, a very nice mediaeval church, and very ancient rocks. And there are some wonderful clean beaches there, with little rock-pools dotted about with little fish, crabs, and starfish in them.

Training 5

They camped in the north-west corner where there is a farmer who lets you camp on a strip of grass next to the beach. It's a lovely sandy beach with lots of driftwood, so they made a fire there and sat around it cooking soup in an old pot that the farmer lent them and baking potatoes in the fire, drank a bottle of whisky, walked up and down collecting nicely shaped pieces of driftwood and watched the sun set on the horizon.

Fantasy Games

My first contact with fantasy role-playing games was in school. I immediately got deeply involved in them, and started to buy books and materials for playing them. I started off by playing around a table, with one person acting as a storyteller, and the others playing characters in the story. They are really in the story, in that they can change the outcome of the story by their actions, which they explain to the storyteller, who in turn tells them what happens, as well as describing to them what they can see and experience in the game's world. So all the players interact within the story, with each other and other characters in the story who the storyteller describes. Usually the players act the part of the "good guys", but not always. All the players need is a piece of paper with a description of their character on it, how strong he or she is, how intelligent, how wise, how fast at running, and things like that.

A year later, I heard about the existence of similar games which are played outside, in the woods, in old castles, and in other similarly atmospheric places. No papers are used, but instead the participants play the part of their characters, wearing costumes and carrying pieces of equipment and weapons - not real ones!- that they might need. You stay in your role for a period of time, anything between a few hours and a few days, and for all of that time you act out your character. It's like living in another age or another world.

The type of characters you can play depends on the setting and the story, but generally, within that, it's nice to be a character with a different personality and different attributes to those you have in real life. You might be a knight, a thief, a magician, an elf, even a monster, in a typical fantasy world. Or if the scenario is a children's story, you might play one of the characters from Alice in Wonderland. We use many themes, such as space, stories from Tolkien's world, or various periods in history.

Last year we used as a setting a very nice castle in Wales, and the story was from the Renaissance times in Italy, so we all had to learn a bit about that period of history in order to prepare for the game. Some people played members of the military or politicians from that time, and we set up the same situation as was at a particular historical date, but, of course, the outcome was not fixed. We just played out history from that point on, but the ending, the conclusion, was completely different to how things happened in real life. I remember I played an Arabian doctor of medicine, with a nice historical costume which was borrowed from a theatre. Most of the game was played by talking - there wasn't so much fighting in that game. I think there was only one fighting person, who played a warrior from Switzerland. Most people played aristocrats, Dukes or royalty, or politicians. The storyteller of that game brought a little magic into the story, to spice it up a bit, and make it more dramatic. So we had a seance in the game - it was actually quite fashionable to have seances in those times. That game was great fun, and it was really interesting to try to make every aspect of the game as authentic as possible, including what we ate and the way we talked.

In some games I played the part of the storyteller, often in conjunction with one or two others. So we made up the story, decided on the setting and the plot. We would introduce the story to some players, who helped us to make the setting, playing monsters or characters with a fixed role according to the storyline, whereas the other players wouldn't know the story, and had to find out what was happening, by interacting with the other characters.

In one adventure we created, the characters were all magicians and sorcerers, and their objective was to build up a tower, a tower of power. The setting was an imaginary country with a kind of Arabian atmosphere, and the participants were all dressed in Arabian costumes, with loose clothes, masks, turbans, and things like that.

Many of our stories are set in different countries of one fantasy world, which is a conglomerate of many different environments. So we have one country which is like Germany in the Middle Ages, a country like Iceland, some hot, desert countries, and things like that. This story was involved with making the building, and fighting against dark powers who wanted to destroy the tower. When I write adventures, I like to put a moral into the story, and this time it was that the source of the magic is a dark source. Not all the magicians recognized this at first, and went on building and gaining power, but in the end they had to recognize that their power was only a part of a dark power, to recognize that to make magic of this kind is too dangerous and uncontrollable. One sorcerer knew that the source of the magic wasn't good, and that there was a dark power underneath the tower which would wake up when there was too much magic in it, but the others didn't believe him, and went on regardless, because they were too lost in the money and politics which was motivating their magic, so they couldn't stop it. After about two days, the dark power became more visible, so we sent people playing monsters and evil creatures creeping around, and in the end the story didn't end well, because the power beneath the tower awoke, and all of the characters had to try to escape, and some died. In such a story it is possible for your character to die. Some people's characters learnt from the events that were taking place around them, but it wasn't like learning from a book, they just started to feel the moral. When you're playing a character, you really become him or her, and you feel the consequences of your actions. It's your adventure.

Fantasy Games

1. When did Nick get involved in fantasy games?
2. What did he start buying?
3. What can characters do in a fantasy game around a table?
4. What does the storyteller do there?
5. What do players need to act their characters?
6. When did Nick hear of the outside games?
7. Where are they played?
8. What do participants need to act their characters?

9. How long can such a game last?

10. What is it like playing such a game?

11. What kind of characters can you play in a typical fantasy world?

12. What kind of themes do they use?

13. What did they use as a setting last year?

14. What was the story like?

15. What did the participants have to do to prepare for the game?

16. Who did they play?

17. What was different from the historical situation?

18. Who did Nick play?

19. What did the storyteller bring into the story?

20. Why was that game such great fun?

21. What did Nick have to do when he played the storyteller?

22. What was one adventure he created about?

23. What was the setting for that story?

24. What was the moral of that adventure?

25. What is the difference between learning from a book and learning from a fantasy game?

Fantasy Games

Training 1

Nick's first contact with fantasy role-playing games was in school. He immediately got deeply involved in them. He started off by playing around a table, with one person acting as a storyteller, and the others playing characters in the story. They can change the outcome of the story by their actions. So, all the players interact within the story.

Training 2

Then Nick heard about similar games which are played in some atmospheric places. The participants play the part of their characters, wearing costumes and carrying pieces of equipment and weapons that they might need. You stay in your role for a period of time, and for all of that time you act out your character. It's like living in another age or another world.

Training 3

The type of characters depends on the setting and the story. You might be a knight, a thief, a magician, an elf, a monster, or a character from Alice in Wonderland. They use many themes, such as space, stories from Tolkien's world, or various periods in history. When you're playing a character, you really become him or her, and you feel the consequences of your actions.

Training 4

Last year they used a castle in Wales as a setting, and the story was from the Renaissance times. Some people played members of the military or politicians from that time, and they set up the historical situation, but the outcome was not fixed. The storyteller of that game brought a little magic into the story, to spice it up a bit. It was really interesting to try to make every aspect of the game as authentic as possible, including what they ate and the way they talked.

Training 5

When Nick writes adventures, he likes to put a moral into the story. Once the characters were all magicians and their objective was to build up a tower of power. And the moral was that the source of the magic is a dark source. In the end the story didn't end well, because the dark power awoke, and some characters died. You could learn from those events, but it wasn't like learning from a book, they just started to feel the moral.

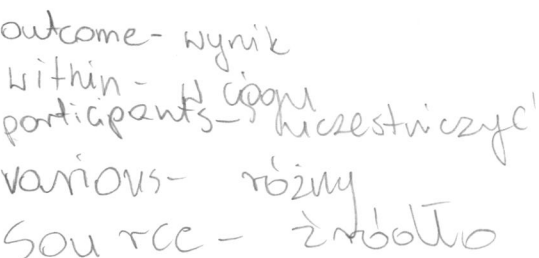

Ramblin' Oer Them There Faerie Hills

I recall a time in my teenage years when I was walking in the mountains, the eastern edge of which roll down into the east coast of Ireland to a place called Newcastle, in County Down. I wasn't walking to get somewhere, I was just walking for the sake of walking through the mountains for four days, because I enjoyed being alone. There were many very magical places, and they all had strange and beautiful names, the cliffs and mountains and rocks. It was a very beautiful place. After four days of just walking in the hills, I felt very clear headed, very cleansed, and when I returned to the so-called "civilized" world it didn't seem so civilized any more, but very dark and dirty instead.

Anyway, as I was walking along, I came to a path which wasn't on the map, but the direction of this path indicated that it seemed to be a more direct route to where I wanted to get to. So I decided I would take the path, and I walked along it for about fifteen minutes, I suppose, and the path came to an end and I found myself on a road. This road was not where I thought I was going to end up. It was, actually, very far away from where I expected to be, so I looked at the map, and I looked at all of the mountains around. I looked at all of the features and the contours, and found out where I was.

I found out that I was three miles from where I had been fifteen minutes ago. Obviously, this was an impossible thing to have happened. So I decided to formulate some theories as to how this could have happened. Maybe my watch was wrong, and it wasn't really fifteen minutes. But it was. It felt like fifteen minutes. Maybe the map was wrong. But it was an Ordnance Survey map. Ordnance Survey maps are not usually that wrong - in fact, they're normally incredibly accurate, as they're taken from aerial photographs.

So I then came up with the possibility that I'd stepped through a black hole in time, which isn't really feasible, because black holes only happen in space, as far as I'm aware. I then thought about the area I was in. It was very desolate region, very untouched by mankind, and there are lots of what logical people call "legends" about faerie (sometimes spelled "fairy") folk, elves and other magical beings, which are very prominent in Irish culture. All of the best Irish mythological heroes are a product of one faerie folk parent and one human parent, often a king of some sort. Also, faerie mounds, lonely hills where the faerie folk live, are common in the local stories, places where humans are somehow unable to visit.

So I wondered if there had been a faerie mound in the middle of this path - or maybe a cluster of them or maybe a whole city, which a mere mortal like myself was not allowed to walk past. So as I walked down the path a quarter of a mile, maybe I was moved by magic over two miles further on, to the last part of the path, so I wouldn't be conscious of walking past the faerie mound.

There are several reasons you could come up with to explain my strange journey, but that one's my favourite, and I think I'll stick with it!

Ramblin' Oer Them There Faerie Hills

1. Where was he walking?

2. What was he walking for?

3. How long was his journey?

4. What was the landscape like?

5. What did he feel like after walking for four days?

6. What did he find?

7. Why did he decide to take that path?

8. How long did he walk along it?

9. Where did he find himself when the path came to an end?

10. Did he expect to get there?

11. How did he find out where he was?

12. How far was that road from where he had been 15 minutes before?

13. What was strange about that little walk?

14. Why did he start speculating on different theories?

15. What was his first theory?

16. Why was he sure that his watch wasn't wrong?

17. What could be another reasonable explanation?

18. Why was it hardly possible that the map was wrong?

19. Why didn't he consider seriously the black hole theory?

20. What was the place he was in like?

21. Who lives in such regions according to the legends?

22. What are faerie mounds?

23. What was his final theory?

24. How did he manage to get to that road so fast then?

25. Which theory is his favourite one?

Ramblin' Oer Them There Faerie Hills

Training 1

He was walking in the mountains, the eastern edge of which roll down to Newcastle. He wasn't walking to get somewhere, he was just walking for the sake of walking through the mountains, because he enjoyed being alone. There were many magical places, and they all had strange and beautiful names, the cliffs and mountains and rocks. It was a very beautiful place.

Training 2

As he was walking along, he came to a path which wasn't on the map, but it seemed to be a more direct route. So he decided he would take the path. He walked along it for about fifteen minutes, and the path came to an end and he found himself on a road. This road was very far away from where he expected to be, so he looked at the map, the mountains around, the features and the contours, and found out where he was.

Training 3

He found out that he was three miles from where he had been fifteen minutes ago. Obviously, this was an impossible thing to have happened. He thought that maybe his watch was wrong, and it wasn't really fifteen minutes. But it felt like fifteen minutes. Then maybe the map was wrong. But it was an Ordnance Survey map and they're normally incredibly accurate, as they're taken from aerial photographs.

Training 4

It was very desolate region, very untouched by mankind. And there are lots of "legends" about faerie folk, elves and other magical beings, which are very prominent in Irish culture. Also, faerie mounds, lonely hills where the faerie folk live, are common in the local stories. Fairie mounds are places where humans are somehow unable to visit.

Training 5

So he wondered if there had been a faerie mound in the middle of this path, which a mere mortal was not allowed to walk past. So as he walked down the path a quarter of a mile, maybe he was moved by magic over two miles further on, to the last part of the path, so he wouldn't be conscious of walking past the faerie mound. There are several reasons you could come up with to explain his strange journey, but that one's his favourite!

The Monastery in Taize

Taize is a little village in the south of France, not far from Lyon. During World War II, a man named Roger Schutz went there, escaping from the north of France which was occupied by German troops, and helping to hide others there who were also fleeing from the invasion. He was a minister of the Protestant church, and he always dreamed of creating a quiet place where people could come just to pray and be at peace. He settled there, and slowly, over the years, was joined by many other men, from all of the different Christian denominations. Those living and working there became greater in number, earning their living working on the land, and living a kind of monastic life, but not according to strict rules. They started to receive regular visits from people who had heard about them, and after a while, some of the residents began to occupy their time by showing visitors around, and looking after their needs. They also helped to organize meetings of like-minded people, where people could come and gather and pray, in many parts of the world.

Now they own a large area there, and every year receive many visits, all year round, from people from all over the world. They get especially many visitors around Easter time and in the summer. At Easter there are usually around ten thousand people there. They have large tents there in which people can stay, and a large church, not a normal church but a large hall with carpet on the floor to sit on, many flowers, and little chairs which support you when you kneel down, which are especially good for meditation. At the front there are some icons and many candles, and a place for an orchestra to sit and play in the prayer meetings there. These meetings always follow the same procedure. First, somebody reads from the Bible. Sometimes, Roger Schutz gives a few thoughts for the day, always very short ones which you can remember and think about. He usually says them in lots of languages, so most of the people there can hear something in their own language.

Then comes the singing, which takes up most of the meeting. They distribute the text of the songs in many languages, with the notes. The songs mostly consist of one very meaningful sentence, which you sing lots and lots of times, which also gives you the opportunity to contemplate its meaning. The musical notation is always scored for four voices, and so you can sing very nice harmonies. The instruments accompany the singing, and always play beautiful variations on the melodic themes.

These main prayer meetings take place three times a day. In between these, you can choose what to do. You can have a silent week there, remaining in silence for a week, in which case you can stay in little houses a short distance away and go down for the prayer meetings if you want to. You can choose to spend a week working there, helping in the kitchens, helping with the cleaning or a variety of other things, or you can be a regular visitor, in which case in the mornings and afternoons you take part in short meetings, in small groups of ten or fifteen people, where people talk about certain topics, about the Bible, or about their lives. Or you can go on walks, as the village is located in beautiful countryside, with little rolling hills, small churches, old houses and not many people. Taize is on the edge of Provence in the south of France, which is always very sunny and has very warm colours.

People usually visit Taize for a week. They start their week on a Sunday and stay until the following Sunday. The size of the contributions they ask for depends on where you come from. If you come from a rich country, such as Switzerland or Austria, you are asked to pay more than if you come from, for example, Hungary or Slovakia. If you are from a well-off country but are relatively poor, and can't afford the rates for your country, you can pay less, according to your means.

So they hold international meetings there all year long. At any time there you can go to talk with the monks there. You can meet people from many different Christian denominations there, and from many different religions. When I was there I met some members of the Hare Krishna movement, Buddhists, Catholics and people from other religions. But I think in their way of thinking the monks are closest to Catholicism. The Pope really likes them, and has a very good relationship with Roger Schutz. If they have big meetings he always sends a letter of support, saying that he likes the idea behind what's going on there.

Meetings take place not only in Taize but also in other places, such as London and Paris, in Europe usually, but not only in Europe, everywhere. People come together, usually at New Year, to pray for the year ahead, or at Easter time. I was in meetings like this in Wroclaw in Poland, in Prague in the Czech Republic, and in Budapest. They were always in the winter time, and many, many people came, and these big towns were just filled up with many thousands of nice, smiling young people from all over Europe.

The inhabitants of these towns could really see the effects of the meetings, with many people on the streets singing and praying and being nice, and a very good atmosphere developed each time. Large food-distribution centres were set up, where the people who came for the meetings could eat together. We were staying with local families, or when there weren't enough host families, in schools.

In Wroclaw I stayed with a family, in Prague I stayed in a monastery, and I was living in Budapest at the time of the meeting there, as, although I was born and raised in England, part of my family are Hungarian. Months before each meeting, young people go to the town where the meeting will happen to organize them. When I was staying in Budapest, we were host to a lovely Polish girl who came to prepare for the meeting there, which was at Christmas, and three or four months before I went with her and helped her to talk to the priests in the church, as I speak quite good Hungarian, to ask if they could talk to their congregations and ask if they would be willing to accommodate guests at the time of the meeting, or if they could let us use the church for the morning prayers. Usually in these meetings, people have breakfast with their host families, then go to a nearby church for morning prayer, then during the daytime go to big meeting centres, in sports halls or places like that. So I helped with that, and that was really nice, then afterwards she stayed with us during the meeting, over Christmas time. She is a very deeply religious person who spent years in Taize as a helper. There are no nuns in Taize, but if you want to stay there for longer than a week you can stay for longer periods as well.

One of the strongest experiences for me at Taize and in the meetings was when everybody gathered to pray together in silence. When my sister and I were in Taize, there weren't so many people there, as it was the beginning of spring, which is not as busy as other times of the year there, but I still spent most of my time in the big church, as I enjoyed these times of sitting and praying in silence greatly. But in the meetings it was a very big experience, to be in a big tent filled with many thousands of people praying in silence, and sometimes the prayers were directed towards something, for example, when we were in Wroclaw it was during the time of the Romanian revolution, so people were very concerned about that. So we all prayed for that, and there was a very strong feeling that all of those people were praying for the same thing. I really believe in the power of prayer. Jesus said that faith can move mountains, and I believe that it can heal the Earth.

The most important idea which has developed in Taize is that you can go to meetings or to Taize, have a great time and get filled up with nice feelings and positive energy, and get some good ideas and inspiration, but then you should go home and start to build up good feelings and beneficial projects there, with your friends, neighbours and family. So if there are ten thousand people in a meeting and they all go home full of enthusiasm and decide to do something, it will really have a positive effect on the world, and make a big change. I think this is a great idea, a wonderful way to really change the world for the better.

The Monastery in Taize

1. What is Taize?
2. Why did Roger Shutz have to escape there?
3. What did he always dream about?
4. Who joined him over the years?
5. What kind of life do they all live?

6. How did it happen that some of them look after the visitors?

7. When do they get especially many visitors?

8. How many people can gather there at Easter?

9. What kind of facilities do they have in Taize?

10. What are the prayer meetings like?

11. What is the main part of such a meeting?

12. Why do songs consist of only one meaningful sentence?

13. How can people from all over the world sing the same songs?

14. How often do prayer meetings take place?

15. What can you do between them?

16. Where can you stay if you have a silent week?

17. Where can you help if you choose to work?

18. What do regular visitors do?

19. Why is it so nice just to go on walks?

20. How long do people usually stay in Taize?

21. How much is the contribution?

22. Where else do the meetings take place?

23. Where do the visitors stay at the international meetings?

24. Who prepares for these meetings?

25. What is a typical day at an international meeting like?

The Monastery in Taize

<u>Training 1</u>

Taize is a little village in the south of France. During World War II, Roger Schutz went there, escaping from the German troops. He was a minister of the Protestant church, and he always dreamed of creating a quiet place for people to pray and be at peace. He settled there, and slowly was joined by people from different Christian denominations. They earn their living working on the land, and live a kind of monastic life, but not according to strict rules.

Training 2

Now they receive a lot of visitors from all over the world. The meetings always follow the same procedure. First, somebody reads from the Bible. Sometimes, Roger Schutz gives a few thoughts for the day. Then comes the singing. The songs mostly consist of one very meaningful sentence, which you sing lots and lots of times. The musical notation is always scored for four voices, and so you can sing very nice harmonies.

Training 3

These main prayer meetings take place three times a day. In between these, you can choose what to do. You can have a silent week there. You can choose to spend a week working there, or you can be a regular visitor and take part in short meetings, in small groups, where people talk about certain topics. Or you can go on walks, as the village is located in beautiful countryside, with little rolling hills, small churches, old houses and not many people.

Training 4

Meetings take place not only in Taize but also in other places. John was in meetings like this in Wroclaw, in Prague, and in Budapest. And a very good atmosphere developed each time. They were staying with local families or in schools. Usually in these meetings, people have breakfast with their host families, then go to a nearby church for morning prayer, then during the daytime go to big meeting centres, in sports halls or places like that.

Training 5

The most important idea which has developed in Taize is that you can go to meetings or to Taize, and get some good ideas and inspiration, but then you should go home and start to build up good feelings and beneficial projects there, with your friends, neighbours and family. This is a great idea and a wonderful way to really change the world for the better.

The Man from the Moon

I first met Alistair on my very first day at University. I was studying architecture, as I had always wanted to be an architect, and Alistair was studying civil engineering. The university had some fancy idea about combining the first years of the architecture and civil engineering courses, so the civil engineers would get some idea about design, and the architects would find out what a brick looked like. So we met on the first day. Those were the days of the student revolutions, so we spent a lot of time marching up and down protesting about things.

In the second year of our studies, we shared a flat with two other students, which was great fun actually. Given that we were four lads living together, we were pretty civilized really. All of the housework was dished out evenly between the four of us, and me and Alistair did all of the shopping and all of the cooking, which totally absolved us of any responsibility for things like cleaning work, which was great by me.

I'll tell you about the worst meal we ever had. Alistair was a very good cook, and I'm not so bad myself, but we were students, and we didn't have too much money, you see, so we were always looking for ways to economize. We experimented one day, attempting to make herring curry. This probably would have been pretty bad to start with, but we decided to add cinnamon. Now, some spice jars have a little grill on top, so only a little comes out, and some don't, but this one didn't and Alistair thought it did, so as he shook the cinnamon over the pot, instead of just a sprinkling the whole lot went in. We tried to eat it, but luckily we were sensible enough to serve it separately to the rice. After one mouthful, somebody said, "This is horrible." We all agreed - it really was disgusting - and ended up only eating rice for supper.

He played guitar at that time with a very good jazz-rock group, and after his degree he moved down to London with them. One night there, he went to bed - he was sleeping in his sleeping bag - and it being quite hot, he had the window open. His room was on the third floor of the house. The next thing he knew was that he was in hospital, because somehow he had managed to fly, or roll, out of the window, in his sleeping bag, and to this day he still doesn't know what happened. The people who lived below him on the second floor saw him falling past their window. The doctors said that he was probably asleep when he hit the ground, because the damage was relatively slight - normally, you'd either die or be paralysed after falling down from a third-floor window. He was badly injured, but it wasn't that serious.

He was in hospital for a long time, where in fact he was "hamster-wheeled." The hospital had got this thing from America for patients who had to stay in bed for a long time. It was like a huge wheel, and his bed was in the middle of the wheel, so he'd lie on his back, and then they'd clamp another bed down on top of him, strap him in, and turn the whole thing over, so he'd be lying on his front, with the other bed on his back. Then they'd take that off of him, and after three hours they'd strap him in again, put the other bed back on, and turn him round again, and again every three hours. The reason for this was that if you lie for a long time in one position it's not very good for your skin to stay in contact with the bed, and you get bed sores, and he couldn't turn over by himself as, with all his injuries, he wasn't able to move. The nurses were very nice, apparently, and gave him lots of Guinness!

Eventually Alistair moved back to Edinburgh, and he went to the Edinburgh Festival, which is a big cultural event that takes place for a couple of weeks every year there, and was asked to do a children's show there. He had bumped into a magician, whose stage name was Magic Bob, who worked in Edinburgh, and wanted someone else to perform with. Now, Alistair had never played for children before, but he sat down and thought, "What can I do? I know, I'll come from the moon!"

So he got this kind of overall, and his wife stitched little stars and moons on it, and he found an old lampshade in the cupboard and put this lampshade on his head, and he made himself into a one-man-band, sitting on top of a drum, with his guitar and a mouth organ and a kazoo, and pretended to be the one-man-band from the moon. I don't know how successful his first concerts were, but they must have inspired him, as he decided to continue in this role and later went on to become very successful. He was very good, as he had a sort of child-like sense of humour. You know, he was not patronizing, as he knew how to think like a child.

There are two common problems with children's entertainers. Firstly, quite often they don't really like playing for children, and are just doing it for the money. The other problem is that they think that children like dragons and castles and princesses and things that they think children would like, when in fact he found that children are often really captivated by everyday things, with perhaps just a bit of magic to make the show a bit spectacular.

Now he goes around and plays in places like village halls, travelling around with his family in a little van, and he's doing quite well from it now. He tends to perform in one area at one time, for example he takes his van to the Outer Hebrides for a week and plays a few times a day there, and then moves on to a different region.

Just before Christmas time he was asked to host a show in a big concert hall in Glasgow, which lasted for a month. That was successful in that he was well paid for it and a lot of people saw him, but he didn't like it very much. It was too big and impersonal, and the contact with the audience wasn't anything like as good as it was in smaller shows, so he's stopped doing such big shows now.

He says that beyond a certain scale, the atmosphere becomes a lot weaker, and he decided he didn't need the money that much. It's understandable really, that he prefers playing for maybe thirty children in a school hall, where he really feels he's communicating with the children, than in a huge hall with one thousand five hundred children.

My children love to see him when we go back home to Scotland, and love listening to his tapes and singing along with them. Being brought up in Hungary, and going to a Hungarian school, they don't have so much exposure to English - my wife's Hungarian and we speak mostly in Hungarian at home - and so they learnt quite a lot of English from him and his tapes. His songs are very educational for youngsters - he sings about the seasons, days of the week and things like that as well as telling funny stories. They see him almost like a cartoon character, as he comes across as somebody very extraordinary.

The Man from the Moon

1. When did Ross first meet Alistair?

2. What were they studying there?

3. How did they make friends?

4. What were Ross and Alistair's household chores?

5. What was their worst meal?

6. What did Alistair do after his degree?

7. What was the strange accident that happened to him one night?

8. Which floor did he live on?

9. What was the most peculiar about that accident?

10. How did the doctors explain his narrow escape?

11. What was interesting about his long stay in hospital?

12. When and where was he first asked to perform for children?

13. Whose idea was that?

14. What character did Alistair decide to perform?

15. What was his fancy dress like?

16. What did he pretend to be?

17. Which musical instruments did his one-man-band play?

18. What did he decide to do after those concerts?

19. Why has he become so successful?

20. What are common problems with children's entertainers?

21. What are children really captivated by?

22. Where does Alistair play now?

23. Where did he host a show just before Christmas?

24. Was his show successful?

25. Why didn't he like it very much himself?

The Man from the Moon

Training 1

Ross first met Alistair at University. They shared a flat with two other students, which was great fun actually. All of the housework was dished out evenly between the four of them, and Ross and Alistair did all of the shopping and all of the cooking. But they always looked for ways to economise and experimented which wasn't always a good idea.

Training 2

Alistar played guitar at that time with a very good jazz-rock group, and after his degree he moved down to London with them. One night there, when he was sleeping in his sleeping bag, he somehow he managed to fly, or roll, out of the window, in his sleeping bag. The doctors said that he was probably asleep when he hit the ground, because the damage was relatively slight.

Training 3

Eventually Alistair moved back to Edinburgh, and was asked to do a children's show there. Alistair had never played for children before, but he sat down and thought he'd come from the moon. So he got this kind of overall with stars on it, and put an old lampshade on his head, and pretended to be the one-man-band from the moon. He was very good, as he was not patronising and had a sort of child-like sense of humour.

Training 4

There are two common problems with children's entertainers. Firstly, quite often they don't really like playing for children. The other problem is that they think that children like dragons and castles and princesses, when in fact Alistair found that children are really captivated by everyday things, with perhaps just a bit of magic to make the show a bit spectacular.

Training 5

Now he goes around and plays in places like village halls, and he's doing quite well from it. Just before Christmas time he was asked to host a show in a big concert hall in Glasgow, which lasted for a month. That was successful, but he didn't like it very much. It was too big and impersonal. Whereas he prefers playing for thirty children in a school hall, where he really feels he's communicating with the children.

Learning Hungarian

A few years ago I met a lovely girl from Hungary, we fell in love, and we married. We decided to live in Hungary, so I was challenged with having to learn the language as soon as possible. I had the possibility to start learning the basics of the language in England at a local evening school, from native speakers, but there was only one lesson a week for two years, which didn't seem to be very much. So when we finally came here to live in Budapest, I couldn't speak fluently, just the basics, no more.

Fortunately I had the possibility to begin working in Hungary as soon as I arrived, working for a company which makes television sets. I'm an engineer by profession, so it was possible to arrange the job beforehand and start straight away. There was quite a funny incident when I first arrived at work, as the woman in the personnel department asked me to sit down, and I couldn't understand her!

They got me a place working in the technology department, where I had an older colleague who could also speak German. I speak a little German, so we could talk, and also a little bit in Hungarian. In the beginning they couldn't find anything for me to do there, so even though I was an employee of this company, and went to the factory every day, I didn't really have any function there. So I enjoyed myself, and talked to my colleagues, and I brought along my Hungarian-English dictionary and used the time to develop my Hungarian.

After half a year, one colleague left the department, and I had to take over his job, which included telephoning, writing letters, and going to the countryside to talk to other employees of the company who were situated there. It was a very difficult time for me, but I couldn't have had a better school than the time I spent there when I arrived. Of course, I consistently made lots of mistakes, but my colleagues helped me. I often had to talk to the other technicians and the workers there in the factory, and also with the staff who were working to my instructions - I also had to prepare operational plans for them to work to, and they were very helpful to me in pointing out my mistakes and rectifying them. After a few years of working there I became fairly fluent in Hungarian, and now I am able to translate between Hungarian and English, and use Hungarian in my everyday life. But this is thanks to having received so much help.

I still don't often speak with my wife in Hungarian, as she speaks English very fluently, very well, but most of our friends are Hungarian, so I use Hungarian a lot in social life. Sometimes I go to theatres and cinemas in Hungarian, and I can understand most of what the people are saying. But I still make mistakes. Very often I try to translate directly from my own language and end up making words and sentences that make absolutely no sense in Hungarian. It's a slow process learning a new language, but I'm continually encouraged as I find myself able to understand more and more words, and handle them better myself.

Learning Hungarian

1. Who did John marry?

2. Why did he have to learn Hungarian as soon as possible?

3. Where did he start learning it?

4. What were the advantages and disadvantages of those courses?

5. Could he speak good Hungarian when they came to live in Hungary?

6. When did he start working in Hungary?

7. What funny incident happened to him on the first day?

8. Who did he work with in the technology department?

9. Which languages did John speak at work?

10. What was peculiar about his first working months?

11. How did he use that period?

12. Why did John have to take over some other colleague's job?

13. What did that job include?

14. What was especially difficult about that job?

15. Why is John grateful for it now?

16. How did his colleagues help him?

17. When did he become fluent in Hungarian?

18. What is he able to do now?

19. Does he often speak with his wife in Hungarian?

20. Who does he speak it with?

21. What about theatre and cinema?

22. Is his Hungarian perfect now?

23. What is his typical problem?

24. Is he improving?

25. Why does he find learning Hungarian encouraging?

Learning Hungarian

<u>Training 1</u>

A few years ago John met a lovely girl from Hungary, they fell in love, and married. They decided to live in Hungary, so he had to learn the language as soon as possible. He had the possibility to start learning the basics of the language in England from native speakers, but there was only one lesson a week for two years. So when they finally came to live in Budapest, he couldn't speak fluently, just the basics, no more.

<u>Training 2</u>

Fortunately he had the possibility to begin working as soon as he arrived, working for a company which makes television sets. He's an engineer by profession, so it was possible to arrange the job beforehand and start straight away. There was quite a funny incident when the woman in the personnel department asked John to sit down, and he couldn't understand her!

Training 3

They got him a place in the technology department, where he had a colleague who could also speak German. So they could talk in German, and also a little bit in Hungarian. In the beginning they couldn't find anything for him to do, and he didn't have any function there. So he enjoyed himself, talked to his colleagues, and used the time to develop his Hungarian.

Training 4

After half a year, one colleague left the department, and John had to take over his job, which included telephoning, writing letters, and going to the countryside to talk to other employees of the company. It was a very difficult time for him, but he couldn't have had a better school. Of course, he consistently made lots of mistakes, but his colleagues were very helpful to him in pointing out his mistakes and rectifying them.

Training 5

After a few years of working there John became fairly fluent in Hungarian, and now he is able to translate between Hungarian and English, and use Hungarian in his everyday life. Most of his friends are Hungarian, so he uses Hungarian a lot in social life. He still makes mistakes, though. It's a slow process learning a language, but he's continually encouraged as he is able to understand more words, and handle them better himself.

A Winter's Tale

The following story took place in January, 1996. My friend Norman invited my brother and me to visit him in Devon, as it was his birthday and he was holding a party at a hotel near his home. I was staying at home with my parents at the time, as it was the end of the Christmas holiday. So we prepared to leave, first making a huge chocolate cake with cream on top for Norman's birthday, and then packing all of the things that we would need for the trip. We borrowed a car for the journey from our father, and packed our instruments, which we thought we might need as Norman is a very enthusiastic musician, like ourselves - my brother brought his bagpipes, his drum, his violin and his viola, and I just brought my fiddle as I only play the fiddle - and packed our sleeping bags, as it was to be a two-day party. It was a very slow journey, as it was snowing heavily, so visibility was low, and some of the roads were very twisty and windy.

Eventually, however, we got there, and it was still light when we arrived. The place where the party was being held was a large modern hotel which also had a wonderful vegetarian restaurant. It also served as a seminar centre, so there were several large seminar rooms there, and it was in one of these that we gathered. Norman was already there, as were some other people, some of them playing instruments. Someone was playing a set of gongs, a few people were playing drums, and one man was sitting on the floor playing a didgeridoo, and it sounded good, so we got out our instruments and joined in. After some nice music, we went down to the restaurant and had a delicious meal, and some other guests arrived. We resumed playing again after eating, and didn't stop until about four in the morning. It was a big room, and we all slept there on the floor in our sleeping bags.

The next morning I wanted to return to London to prepare some work for University, but my brother wanted to stay another day, so I asked the other people at the party and found some people who were going to London in a Volkswagen minibus, one of these small nine-seaters.

First we drove to Norman's to pick up some things, and it seemed to take ages hanging around there before everybody was ready to go - I think it was half past four by the time we left- and so we left quite late. Then we had to go to another house nearby to collect something for an Australian guy who was travelling with us, who lives in London, and this also took an hour or so as it was a very slow drive through some heavy snow. But eventually we got on the road to London.

It seemed like just a normal journey back, if rather dark and cold and snowy. But after about thirty miles, as we were travelling homeward, some cars overtook us, as we were going quite slowly, and there must have been some ice or hard snow attached to the bottom of one of the cars which had come loose, because something flew towards the windscreen and it smashed.

We were so shocked, there was such a loud noise. I was lying in the back of the van. The seats of the van could be adjusted to drop down flat and make beds, so we had put them all down and five of us were lying down in the back in our sleeping bags, because it was so cold as the heating didn't work, and the other three sat in the front. We were listening to some music on the car stereo and suddenly this loud crashing noise came, and we saw that the windscreen had smashed. In the centre of the windscreen there were long shards of glass, and at the outside it had broken into many tiny cubes, so the driver couldn't really see anything.

So we pulled off of the main road and pushed all of the little pieces of glass outside, placing a blanket inside so no glass could fall into the car. Some people driving by saw that we were in trouble, stopped and asked if we needed some help, so we asked them if they had anything to put on it, and they gave us a sheet of clear plastic, but eventually we decided not to use it as the wind would just blow it off again, and if it went into the driver's face it could be dangerous. We asked them if they knew where the next garage was, they told us, and we bade them good-bye.

When we arrived at the garage, which was about ten miles further along the road, we were disappointed to find that it was closed, because it was Sunday evening. That was bad luck, because it was a special Volkswagen garage, and had they been open we probably could have got a new windscreen there. Nevertheless, it was closed, but there was a telephone there, so we called an emergency car service, the AA, or Automobile Association, which the driver was a member of, and they told us, "We can send some people out to put a sheet of plastic over the windscreen." We said, "No, it's okay, we can do that by ourselves, thanks."

So we drove all the way to London with no windscreen. It was really cold, even in our sleeping bags. We ate a lot of chocolate to try to get some energy, but it didn't really help. It was freezing. Luckily, when we got to the outskirts of the city, I phoned an Aunt of mine who lives near there and she told us to come straight away. She has a large garage, so we could put the bus there for one or two days until Richard, the driver, could find somebody to fix the windscreen, and we went in and sat by the fire, watched videos and drank a lot of hot tea, and stayed there for the night. It was so nice to be inside in the warm after such a long cold journey!

A Winter's Tale

1. When did this story take place?
2. Where were John and his brother invited?
3. What did they make for Norman's birthday?
4. Who did they borrow a car from?
5. Why did they pack their instruments, too?
6. Did they get to the party on time?
7. What was going on when they arrived?
8. Which instruments were Norman's guests playing?
9. What did John and his brother do?
10. What did they all do after some music?

11. Did they play some more music that night?

12. Where did they all sleep?

13. Why did John want to leave the next morning?

14. Why couldn't he go in his father's car?

15. Who did he find to solve the problem?

16. Why did they leave so late?

17. What happened after about thirty miles on the road?

18. What were most of the passengers doing at that moment?

19. Why did they have to pull off the road?

20. What did the people passing by give them?

21. Why didn't they want to use the plastic sheet at first?

22. Why couldn't they have the windscreen changed?

23. What did they have to do in the end?

24. What was their journey to London like?

25. What did they have to do when they got to the outskirts of London?

A Winter's Tale

Training 1

In January, 1996 Norman invited John's brother and John to his birthday party at a hotel in Devon. So they made a huge chocolate cake with cream on top for Norman's birthday, and then packed all of the things for the trip. They also packed their instruments, as Norman is a very enthusiastic musician, like themselves. It was a very slow journey, as it was snowing heavily, and some of the roads were very twisty and windy.

Training 2

When they eventually arrived, Norman and some guests were already there. Someone was playing a set of gongs, a few people were playing drums, so they got out their instruments and joined in. After some nice music, they went down to the restaurant and had a delicious meal. They resumed playing again after eating, and didn't stop until about four in the morning. It was a big conference room, and they all slept there on the floor in their sleeping bags.

Training 3

The next morning John wanted to return to London, but his brother wanted to stay another day. So John found some people who were going to London in a minibus. It seemed like just a normal journey back, if rather dark and cold and snowy. But after about thirty miles, some cars overtook them, and something flew towards the windscreen and it smashed.

Training 4

In the centre of the windscreen there were long shards of glass, and at the outside it had broken into many tiny cubes, so the driver couldn't really see anything. So they pulled off of the main road. Some people driving by saw that they were in trouble, stopped and gave them a sheet of clear plastic. They told them where the nearest garage was, but when they arrived at the garage, it was closed.

Training 5

So they drove all the way to London with no windscreen, they had to put a sheet of plastic instead. It was freezing. Luckily, when they got to the outskirts of the city, John phoned an Aunt of his who lives near there. They went in and sat by the fire, drank a lot of hot tea, and stayed there for the night. It was so nice to be inside in the warm after such a long cold journey!

New Hope

When I finished high school, I couldn't go on to college to continue my studies, as I didn't obtain good enough grades in my O-levels. I wanted to learn to be a teacher for vision-impaired or handicapped children, but as I couldn't gain admittance to college I started working in a health-care home for deeply mentally retarded children. Whilst there, I met a boy who was vision-impaired and hearing-impaired, almost completely deaf and blind, and I started thinking: "How much can this boy feel from the world around him?" I felt that if nobody would teach him, he would never really start to learn anything, never be able to really interact with the world, and never come out of his very closed, isolated state. He wasn't interested at all in the world around him, which I could understand, as he couldn't see or hear anything of it.

Later, I was able to afford to go to a training college for special needs teachers, and there I started to learn special techniques for teaching vision-impaired people, and for teaching mentally retarded children. For the third and fourth years of the course, a special educator came from the US who wanted to find some people who were interested in the deaf/blind topic. I was very interested in that, as was one of my colleagues. We started to go around the country visiting special health-care homes for mentally retarded children, and tried to find other deaf/blind people, and we worked with this American woman, who helped us to discover teaching methods for the deaf/blind.

I knew that there is a Catholic school for the blind in Budapest, and after finishing the college I visited it, and found there a deaf/blind boy from Budapest who needed a teacher, so I went there and started to work with him. During the same period, I met some more children and adults who had lost their sense of sight and hearing, and we got some support to organize ways of trying to help them and their families. We organized summer camps, for the children and their families, and tried to arrange for interpreters to be available when needed, for example, for when they needed to go to an office, or for a haircut, for things like that. Also, we tried to find better institutions for them, to find the best places for them to be trained.

For teaching the children to communicate, we first try to use natural gestures, and the sign-language that the deaf use. However, as they can't see, we hold their hands in the different positions, making the gestures through their hands, holding their hands and making the signs with them. For example, the sign for eating is touching the mouth, so to communicate about eating, first we hold the deaf/blind person's hand, and together touch his or her mouth. Then he can have a snack, or something like that. Later on, he doesn't need to have the teacher's hand there, he can do the gestures alone, when he wants to have a snack, for example. We teach them in this way, gesture by gesture. The gesture for drinking is pretending to hold a cup and pouring it into the mouth, and the one for sleeping is putting the hands underneath the head like a pillow. Another example - one of my students likes very much to eat onions, which smell very much so the sign for an onion is turning the hand before the nose, to try to symbolize smelling something.

So these basic things are learnt first, and later on, if they are clever, they can learn Braille, which is special writing which blind people can read with their fingertips. When they've learned this, they are able to read and write. One of my students has just started to learn Braille. He very much likes to eat apples and cheese. We have cards with letters and signs on them, and we begin with each letter being represented by something which starts with that letter, so we introduce the letter A with the apple card, which he has to find if he wants to eat an apple. When he wants to eat cheese, he must find the C card, which means cheese, and when he wants cheese and apple together he picks both of them. Later on, we introduce cards with small words on them. With these, he finds out the words for the table, the chair, the classroom, the window, and things like this. He has to read the card, and then go to the table, the window, or whatever. But for the first stage, we just have letters, with every letter meaning something - A for apple, B for balloon, C for cheese, etc. This is the method for completely blind children. Some have some partial, or "restive" vision, so they can learn with large print, learning normal writing and reading using the normal alphabet.

If they became deaf/blind when they were older we can use different methods. If they were blind before, they may have already learned to read Braille, and they can speak, so it's much easier. We have a special method to "write" Braille letters into their hands, by putting fingers onto different positions of the hand, with each position signifying a different letter, in order to communicate to them. Those people who were deaf before they lost their sight mostly already know the sign-language of the deaf, so they can use that to communicate, and to speak to them the interpreter makes the signs with their hands. Deaf/blind adults can often read the signs by lightly touching the interpreter's hands and watching the way they move. They can also learn Braille, or they can learn the manual alphabet, in which every letter has a different hand signal, a different way of holding the hands. They can read this by holding out their hand, with the interpreter touching the symbols against their palms. They soon become familiar with the feeling of each sign.

I know a man who was a normal child when he was born, but lost his sight at the age of six. Before that he had some problems with his vision, but he had an operation on his eyes which helped to correct them, but when he was six, after another operation, he lost his sight altogether, and so became totally blind. He went to the school for the blind to study, and after finishing school he went on a special course to learn to work at a telephone operating exchange - you know, where you can call and say, "Hi, can you put me through to 1673477?" or something like that. This is a common form of employment for blind people. So, he was doing that as work, and in his free time he liked to listen to different channels of the radio, comparing the different ways of presenting the news on different channels. He started to have some problems with his hearing, so he got an electronic hearing-aid, with which he could hear clearly for a while, but when he was thirty-five years old he lost his hearing altogether. He had to leave his job, and he went to a special institution. He got very depressed, as he didn't know what to do next, or how to live.

However, there is now a new hope, as in May he will have an operation, to receive a special kind of hearing aid called a cochlea implant, in which electrodes are attached to the nerves in the ear which are responsible for hearing. These electrodes give different signals to the nerve, depending on how much audio input they receive, which are transmitted by the nerves to the brain. With this kind of hearing-aid, which is quite a new system, they can hear again, and after a while getting used to it people can understand speech, so maybe after some time he will be able to understand the radio, and things like that. So, he's really excited now, as he's waiting for this operation, and also a bit nervous about how much he'll be able to hear. We're hoping for the best.

We've already had some success with these hearing-aids. I met a twenty-four year old girl who lost her hearing when she was eighteen. She's had this implant for two years, and now she can understand speech quite well, and can hear when somebody is coming. She can only hear in one ear, as they don't put them in both ears as it's quite a big, expensive operation, but later on, it often happens that the hearing on the other side comes back a bit by itself, that the nerve starts to work again. It depends, of course, in which part of the ear the problem is.

The implants can also be used by children who have never been able to hear before. Now experts think that in badly hearing impaired or deaf children it's better to have this kind of implant when they are very young, one or two years old, so that they can learn speech together with other children. I've never met such a child, I've only read about them in articles and books.

New Hope

1. Why couldn't Helen go on to college after high school?

2. What did she want to be?

3. Where did she start working?

4. Who did she meet while working there?

5. What did she feel about that boy?

6. Where did she go to continue her studies?

7. Who did the special educator look for?

8. Were there any people interested in deaf/blind topic?

9. How did the woman teach them teaching methods for the deaf/blind?

10. Who did Helen start to work with after the college?

11. What did they organize for deaf/blind people?

12. What else did they try to do to help them?

13. What do teachers use to teach the deaf/blind to communicate?

14. Why can't they teach them in the same way as they do with the deaf?

15. What do teachers do to show the children the signs?

16. What are some typical gestures of this language?

17. What can these children learn later?

18. What can children do after they have learned Braille?

19. How do they teach Braille to the deaf/blind?

20. Why is it easier to work with the people who became deaf/blind later?

21. What can be a new hope for the deaf/blind?

22. How can the electrodes in the implant restore hearing?

23. Will the operated start to understand speech after the operation?

24. Why can't you have an implant in both ears?

25. When is the best time to operate deaf/blind children?

New Hope

Training 1

When Helen finished high school, she wanted to learn to be a teacher for vision-impaired or handicapped children. So she started working in a health-care home for mentally retarded children. Whilst there, she met a boy who was almost completely deaf and blind. She felt that if nobody would teach him, he would never be able to really interact with the world.

Training 2

Later, she went to a training college for special needs teachers, and there she started to learn special techniques for teaching vision-impaired people. With a special educator Helen started to go around the country trying to find other deaf/blind people, and they worked with this educator, who helped them to discover teaching methods for the deaf/blind.

Training 3

They first try to use natural gestures, that is they hold their hands in the different positions, and make the signs with them. Later on, they can learn Braille, which is special writing which blind people can read with their fingertips. First they introduce letters, for example, 'A' with the apple card, 'C' with the cheese card, etc. Later on, they introduce cards with small words on them.

Training 4

However, there is now a new hope, that is an operation to receive a special kind of hearing aid implant, in which electrodes are attached to the nerves in the ear. These electrodes give different signals to the nerve, which are transmitted by the nerves to the brain. With this kind of hearing-aid, which is quite a new system, they can hear again, and after a while getting used to it people can understand speech.

Training 5

They've already had some success with these hearing-aids. A twenty-four year old girl's had this implant for two years, and now she can understand speech quite well. The implants can also be used by children who have never been able to hear before. Now experts think that it's better to have this kind of implant when they are very young, one or two years old, so that they can learn speech together with other children.

Lone Hitch-Hiker

It was early in November, and I was in Freiburg, in the south of Germany, near the Swiss border. I'd been there for three months, working with an ecological organization which was setting up a music and exhibition tour around Europe. It was called SET, the "Sustainable Europe Tour", and it was about to continue at the beginning of June. I was applying for sponsorship, and writing to different organizations in different countries asking what they could offer for the tour to go there. It was all about sustainable energy, things like how to use your car less, and suggesting and demonstrating many other ways of living with a lower level of energy consumption, and using cleaner energy sources such as wind-power, wave-power and solar-power. It also featured exhibitions about the different sustainable villages and communities around Europe, Permaculture, and things like that. Anyway, after about three months I decided that I had been there long enough, and wanted to go somewhere else.

So I tried to decide where I should go. I didn't want to go back to England or Scotland, but whilst in Poland in August I had met two people from Budapest in Hungary, who had invited me over to stay there for a while, so I decided that that was the perfect option. Now at this time I had a car, and I also had a lot of recording equipment and things. However, I did not have the money for the petrol to take the car, so I decided to hitch-hike, which turned out to be not necessarily the best idea.

For some reason, I started hitch-hiking at about two o'clock in the morning, and I had a rather uneventful journey through Germany. I got to Salzburg at three o'clock the next day - I think it was a Saturday afternoon - twelve and a half hours later. So I went out onto the motorway in Salzburg, and held out my sign, which said, in big bold letters, BUDAPEST. I waited. And I waited. Now, when I set out, I had a bag full of clothes, but by the time I got a lift, rather late in the night, my bag was empty, as it was getting cold and all my clothes were on my body. The further east I travelled, the deeper the snow got, and the colder it got.

Eventually I got a lift halfway to Vienna, where I again got out at a service station, and waited quite a long time to try and find a lift. I eventually found someone who saw my sign and said, "Yes, we're going that way. You can come with us to Budapest." Now, what they didn't tell me was that they were towing a van across the border, and that they in fact had come from Hamburg, in the North of Germany, and were going to Romania, towing this van all of the way. But they had got this far. So I got in the van, in the back of the one which was being towed, and, of course, it had no heating in it, as it had no engine in it.

The night went on, and we eventually arrived at the Hungarian border, where everybody was speaking different languages, none of which I understood, Romanian and Hungarian. There was the man who was towing the van, the man who was in the van that was being towed, and the customs officials. The problem, I found out, was that the Hungarian customs office would not allow this person to tow this van into the country, and there was a lot of arguing and shouting. It was very cold, and I was very tired, as this was the second night that I hadn't slept, and the second night that I'd been out in the cold, as well.

What eventually happened was they had to leave the van being towed at the border, and they all got into the other van, and drove across the border, while me and the other man who owned the van being towed had to walk across the border. Now it was the middle of the night, and there was nobody about, and we walked across the little side road around the place where the lorries go through - there was nobody there, and it was very dark, and all of a sudden a figure jumped out in front of us with a gun, and pointed it at us. We raised our hands, and said, "We're not doing anything", and he had a look at our passports and saw that they had been stamped, so he allowed us to continue walking on through, and we got into the other van and drove to the nearest garage, in Hungary.

I didn't have a clue where I was, and it was still dark and bitterly cold, and the snow was very deep, so I got out of the van, and the person whose van was being towed got into another lorry and disappeared. So I stood freezing at the all-night station, and begged to go into the corridor and warm myself on the heater, which I was grudgingly allowed to do.

As six o'clock in the morning arrived and the sun was rising, more people arrived to work at the petrol station, and one man came in and looked at me and asked, "What are you doing here?" I said, "I want to go to Budapest", showing him the sign. He said, "Okay, I will go and ask some of the people in the station if they will take you." He went and asked several people, and kept on asking people, if they would take me, but nobody would. Nobody seemed to be going to Budapest. It was only a hundred and fifty kilometres away, but it didn't look like I was going to get there.

So I waited at the entrance to the station with my little sign, and cars went past, and more cars went past, and still I had no luck. A few hours later, a lorry arrived at the service station with a van on it. It was the van that had not been allowed through customs at the border the night before. They all got out of the van, and said, "Would you like to come to Budapest?" again, and I, of course, said, "Yes, anything to get out of here." So I got into the van and was towed to the outskirts of Budapest, where I got out of the van feeling very pleased with myself that I had made it.

I waited for a bus, and when one arrived, I asked to be taken to the centre of the town. The bus driver said yes, and charged me money, and when he signalled to me I asked if we were in the centre, and he said, "Igen", which I understood to mean yes. I went straight to the telephone, and telephoned my friend. The phone rang, but nobody answered. Now, this person was expecting my arrival the night before, and I concluded that they were no longer in.

Feeling rather upset, and still very cold, I went to a coffee shop and drank expresso coffee. I sat next to the heater and warmed myself up, and as I was starting to get a bit warmer I tried to phone again. Eventually I got through to my friend, who was completely dismayed as they had been in all morning, but the phone had been dropped on the floor, and the ringer had been accidentally switched off, so that they couldn't hear the phone ringing. They asked, "Where are you?", and as I didn't know I gave the name of the street and described my surroundings, and my friend said, "I haven't a clue where you are but you're certainly not in the centre! But I'll get the map and try to find it." Eventually they found the map, found the place, and came to collect me, and I've been here in Budapest ever since. I haven't hitch-hiked again, and don't intend to!

Lone Hitch-Hiker

1. Where was Daniel in November?
2. What was he doing there?
3. Why did he decide to leave Freiburg?
4. Where did he want to go?
5. Why didn't he travel by car?
6. What time did he start hitch-hiking?
7. What was his journey through Germany like?
8. What time did he get to Salzburg?
9. How did he show where he wanted to go?
10. Why did he have to put on all his clothes?
11. Where did he get a lift from Salzburg?
12. Where did he wait to find a lift farther?
13. What kind of vehicle did he get a lift in?
14. What was the trouble with the van?
15. What time did they arrive at Hungarian border?
16. Why did he have to cross the border on foot?
17. Who did they meet while they were crossing the border?
18. Where did he spend that night?
19. How did he manage to keep more or less warm?

20. When did he start waiting for the lift the next day?

21. How long did it take him to find someone going to Budapest?

22. Who were these people?

23. Where did he get off the van?

24. Why couldn't his friend come and collect him right then?

25. Does Daniel intend to hitch-hike again?

Lone Hitch-Hiker

Training 1

After about three months in Freiburg, Daniel decided that he had been there long enough, and wanted to go somewhere else. In August he had met two people from Budapest in Hungary, who had invited him over to stay there, so he decided that that was the perfect option. As he did not have the money for the petrol to take the car, he decided to hitch-hike.

Training 2

He had an uneventful journey through Germany. He got to Salzburg and went out onto the motorway, and held out his sign, which said BUDAPEST. He waited and waited. By the time he got a lift, his bag was empty, as it was getting cold and all his clothes were on him. The further east he travelled, the deeper the snow got, and the colder it got.

Training 3

Eventually he got a lift halfway to Vienna, and then he waited quite a long time to find a lift. He eventually found someone who was towing a van to Budapest, so he got in the cold van. Late at night they eventually arrived at the Hungarian border. But the Hungarian customs office would not allow to tow this van into the country. It was very cold, and Daniel was very tired, as this was the second night that he hadn't slept and had been out in the cold.

Training 4

So he had to walk across the border. He arrived freezing at the all-night station, and begged to go into the corridor and warm himself on the heater. The next day he waited at the entrance to the station with his little sign, and all the cars went past. A few hours later, a lorry arrived with the same van on it. So he got into it and was towed to the outskirts of Budapest.

Training 5

He waited for a bus, and when one arrived, he asked to be taken to the centre of the town. Then he went straight to the telephone, and phoned his friend. The phone rang, but nobody answered. Feeling rather upset, and very cold, he went to a coffee shop and drank expresso coffee. Then he tried to phone again. Eventually he got through to his friend, who came to collect him. He hasn't hitch-hiked again, and doesn't intend to!

Narrow Escape

I spent last summer in Israel visiting a friend of mine. This friend was studying in Israel at that time, in Beer Sheeva, in a religious Jewish school where they usually study the Torah and other holy books of the Jews. When I arrived at the airport, he was waiting there to collect me, to take me to Jerusalem. We decided to hitch-hike all through the trip as we didn't have too much money, and Israel is a fairly expensive country, and it worked really well - we were very successful.

In Jerusalem I stayed in a place called Heritage House, which is also a religious place for Jews, and if you're Jewish, as I am, you can go there and stay there for free, and you can also find good company, nice people there - it's a bit like a youth hostel. Although it's a religious place, you don't have to strictly keep all the rules of Judaism to stay there. In fact, a lot of people only go there for the nice company, and because it's free. If you want, they will organize courses for you on all kinds of Jewish cultural subjects, such as the Hebrew language, studying the holy books, and things like that. But I didn't go for any of these courses, because I only had three weeks in Israel, for the whole trip, and I didn't feel like spending all of the time there.

Instead, I just went for walks in Jerusalem with my friend. Originally we wanted to go to museums as well, and other places, but then we decided not to, first because of the money, and second because I had never had the chance before to just walk around Jerusalem, and not be told where to go and what to do. I had been to Israel before, but each time I was with organized groups, and this time I had a chance to go to the Arabic market, which I'd never been able to do before, and it was wonderful there. I think it holds the real atmosphere of Jerusalem.

I don't know, but I think it must look and feel exactly the same now as it did hundreds or thousands of years ago. That's one place in Israel where I think you really don't have to be afraid of anything. Everybody is really friendly, in the old city, and it's wonderful that Jews and Arabs can live there together. At least it appears so. Actually, I spent most of my time in Jerusalem in the old city. I had a chance to go down to the Western Wall every day, which is really special, because most of the people who go to Jerusalem just go to the Wall for one day - you know, it's like a tourist attraction, they visit it and see it and try to feel the atmosphere there in one hour, and it never works, at least not for me.

Whenever I go to places - cathedrals, museums or whatever - and I know that I should be impressed, and feel what it's like to be there, I almost never do. If you go there every evening for a few days you can catch the atmosphere, and you start to understand that for a lot of people it's a part of their daily lives, their daily routine, to go and pray there.

While I was there, I met a Hasidic family. The Hasidim are very religious, strictly religious orthodox Jews, who originally come from Eastern Europe. They keep traditions very strongly, not just Biblical traditions, but also the ways of dressing, ways of talking, and other things which are not part of their religion, but are part of their East European culture. It's very strange sometimes, because, for example, they wear long coats and big fur hats, which seem quite funny in Israel, in such a hot country, but they see it as part of keeping their traditions alive, their cultural identity. They say that if you adopt ways from the new civilization, you somehow get further from God. So they're very strict on these things, and they don't usually like to meet other people of different backgrounds, because they know it's a big temptation nowadays for the young people in their community to take on different ways from modern society. So they're very careful about this.

But on Friday evenings, at the beginning of the Sabbath, which is an important part of Jewish religion, they invite other people to visit them and eat with them, admittedly to attract them to their religion, and they cook a big meal, and you become a part of the family for that evening. You can talk about religion and their way of life, or your way of life, with them, and they make a really warm, open, friendly atmosphere. It was very interesting, because I experienced a lot of things that I'd heard of but never seen, for example that women and men don't even sit in the same room, and that the father of the family, when blessing his own children, does not touch the daughters, but puts a handkerchief on top of their heads so that his hand doesn't meet their heads. It's a bit strange, but it was interesting to see that people actually live this way. I think this was the most exciting part of my visit to Jerusalem, as I'd never had the chance to do these things before.

I went afterwards to the north of Israel, which is very different from the other areas of the country - it even looks very different, not so Mediterranean but more like the central part of Europe, with big trees and things. A lot of Israelis go there, as they find it very romantic, as you can't really find big trees, and especially not forests, in any other part of Israel.

I was in the Northwest, on a kibbutz. We had to work for four hours a day, and I worked in the garden. Everyone visiting there had a sort of family to visit. In that kibbutz they still raised the children in communal houses, so the children didn't stay with their families but stayed in a place like a sort of kindergarten where they spent all the morning, and the night, and they only went to see their family for a few hours in the afternoon. Everybody in the kibbutz, especially the older ones, seemed really convinced that this was the way to bring up children, which was really difficult to understand. They said that the reason for this was that you bring up a child to make him or her part of a community; you won't spend all of your life with your immediate family, with your father and mother, so you have to be brought up in a way that makes you feel part of the community, and later on of society. So we had a kind of temporary family there, who we went to visit in the afternoons, and they really did treat us like their children. I had been there before on an earlier visit. I could never live in a kibbutz, I'm sure. It's too closed for me, too small, but there was something really special about it which I've never experienced anywhere else.

When I returned there after five years, everyone that I had met there before, even for only one hour, greeted me as if I really belonged there, and they were really interested in what had been happening to me, and remembered all the things that I did there. It was really like going home, exactly like going home after a long time to your own village or to your own country.

After that I went to Egypt, with my friend, and we spent a few days there, in Sinai, by the sea, which was really beautiful. We swam a lot there, and it was so beautiful to see under the water with a snorkel, looking at all the different coloured fish and corals. It's like another world down there. We stayed in a village called Dahab, where there were a lot of restaurants, but not like normal restaurants, as all they had were cushions on the floor to sit on, and very short tables, and a shade up above, and it was very nice because you could just spend all day lying there if you wanted to, listening to the sound of the sea and enjoying a bit of shade from the desert heat.

I can't explain how beautiful it is there. You just have to go there and feel it, the peace and the space and the silence. The whole area is just desert and sea, with many changing colours in the sand and the mountains as the sun passes over, and millions of stars at night in a crystal clear sky. We stayed in a very simple little hut, which we rented very cheaply from the Bedouin restaurant owner, with just a bed in it, which served to keep the flies off and give a bit of shade in the morning.

Anyway, after a few days we had to leave Dahab, and we wanted to go back to Jerusalem, so we decided to try to hitchhike from the border of Israel, on the edge of Eilat. We were very very lucky, as the first car that came past us stopped. The driver said that he could take us all the way to Jerusalem, and we were delighted, as we hadn't expected such good fortune. What's more, the driver was very friendly and nice. It turned out that he was a Christian Arab, and it was a little bit difficult to communicate with him, as he didn't speak much English or Hebrew and we didn't speak Arabic, but somehow we managed. He was a very dynamic, lively person who was fond of his country, and every few minutes would attempt to express how greatly he loved Israel. He gave us food and drink as if we were his guests. It's quite typical, if you are with Arabic people, that they want to make sure you are always completely satisfied, with enough to eat and drink, and we had everything we needed there in the back seat.

Then we stopped at The Dead Sea, just to have a quick swim, and he was telling us all about his family and his work, and telling us a lot about the country. He really knew a lot about different things and places to go. We were having a very enjoyable journey, as it was fascinating to talk to him, and we felt very confident. The only problem was that he was so dynamic that he couldn't drive at less than 140 kilometres per hour, which didn't feel a lot in the middle of the desert. We weren't afraid at first, but the other thing he did, which he shouldn't have done, was that he overtook other cars quite dangerously, even when there was only a small space on the other side of the road to pass by.

When we got to 40 kilometres from Jerusalem we thought, "In these last 40 kilometres nothing can happen", but we were wrong. In the very last moment before arriving in the city, I don't know exactly what happened, but it seemed that he wanted to overtake a car, so he moved out into the road, and suddenly he saw a car coming in the opposite direction. And he somehow lost his head and swerved left, off the road. He lost control of the car and we fell into the ditch. The car kept moving, and we turned over twice, and then the car landed on its roof. It all happened very quickly. It was very strange. I remember that the only thing I said, when we started to turn over, was that I told this friend to hold on. I don't know why I remember that actually, as I can't remember anything else about it. My friend's first thought was to quickly get out of the car, as it smelled of petrol, and he thought after watching so many stupid action movies that the next thing that would happen would be that the car would explode. So we got out of the car, and we saw that the driver was also getting out, so we ran away. People stopped by the road to see if we were okay, and that was when we realized just how dangerous it had been, as all of the people who saw the accident were amazed to see that we were still alive, and were saying how lucky we were. I was all covered in blood, as was my friend's face, but it turned out luckily that he had just cut his ear slightly. It could have been fatal, and it was just a miracle that we all survived relatively unharmed.

Narrow Escape

1. Where did Joshua spend last summer?

2. How did the friends get to Jerusalem?

3. Where did Joshua stay in Jerusalem?

4. Why do most people stay there?

5. What kind of courses can you do in Heritage House?

6. Why didn't Joshua go for any of them?

7. Why didn't they go to museums?

8. Had Joshua been to Jerusalem before?

9. Why was this visit special?

10. What kind of places did he visit in Jerusalem this time?

11. Why did he find important to go to the Western Wall every day?

12. What kind of family did he meet in Jerusalem?

13. Why are the Hasidim so special among the Jews?

14. How did Joshua happen to meet this family at all?

15. What did they do when he visited them?

16. Why is the north of Israel different from other areas?

17. Where did he stay in the north?

18. What did he find strange about the life in that kibbutz?

19. What was their typical day in the kibbutz like?

20. What impressed him most of all there?

21. Where did Joshua and his friend go after that?

22. What did they do at the seaside?

23. How did they want to get back?

24. What happened to them when they wanted to overtake a car?

25. What was miraculous about the accident?

Narrow Escape

Training 1

Joshua spent last summer in Israel visiting a friend of his. Originally they wanted to go to museums and other places, but then they decided not to. As Joshua had been to Israel before with organised groups he had never had the chance before to just walk around Jerusalem, and, for example, go to the Arabic market, and it was wonderful there.

Training 2

Actually, he spent most of his time in Jerusalem in the old city. He had a chance to go down to the Western Wall every day, which is really special. He also met a Hasidic family. The Hasidim are strictly religious orthodox Jews, and he experienced a lot of things that he'd heard of but never seen, for example, that women and men don't even sit in the same room.

Training 3

He went afterwards to the north of Israel, which is very different from the other areas of the country. Joshua was in the Northwest, on a kibbutz. The children there stayed in a sort of kindergarten where they spent all the morning, and the night, and they only went to see their family in the afternoon. They also had a temporary family, who they went to visit in the afternoons. And they had to work for four hours a day.

Training 4

After that they went to Egypt and spent a few days by the sea. They swam a lot there, and it was so beautiful to see under the water with a snorkel. They stayed in a very simple little hut in a village, where there were a lot of unusual restaurants with just cushions on the floor, very short tables, and a shade up above. On their way back they decided to hitchhike from the border of Israel. The first car that came past them stopped.

<u>Training 5</u>

However, the driver overtook other cars rather dangerously. Once when he moved out into the road, he suddenly saw a car coming in the opposite direction. And he swerved left, off the road. He lost control of the car and they fell into the ditch. The car turned over twice, and then landed on its roof. They got out quickly, but the car didn't explode anyway. It could have been fatal, and it was just a miracle that they all survived unharmed.

Music Makes the World Go Round

I work with mentally handicapped children, mostly Down's syndrome children, aged between five and thirty, and have done for a few years now. I have always observed how much they love music, and, being a musician myself, always wanted to find a way to teach them to play. All the books I ever read, however, and all the experts I ever talked to, told me that it was impossible, that in Down's syndrome kids the part of the brain which is responsible for creating music didn't function properly. However, I found out that this was only really considered true until about ten years ago, when a German called Dr. Ulrich began very enthusiastically to teach the mentally handicapped children he was working with to play instruments. He says that not only can these children play music, but that they should, as it's very very good for them, and they enjoy it enormously.

He has designed a great variety of instruments that the children can play, and proposes that the main problem has always been not with the children, but with the system of notation used to write music down. This is not only difficult to learn for mentally handicapped people, he says, but for many normal people as well. So he has created a special system of writing music down which uses many different shapes and colours to represent the pitch and duration of the notes, instead of the usual mass of little black dots, and it's really very good.

Now he has a school, in Germany, where the children have three music lessons a day. The first lesson, in the morning, is a very happy, joyful session of singing and dancing, which all the pupils attend together, and the other two lessons, which take place in the afternoon, are for teaching this special new system of reading music and learning to play the instruments. You could say that this is too much for the children, but it isn't, because they like it so much, and not only do they have fun learning and playing, but they have a lot of success with it as well, and really feel a sense of achievement. Also, it is not only good for developing their musical ability, but also their physical co-ordination, counting, reading and concentration abilities, the teaching of each of which becomes much easier with music.

This man is so dedicated to his work, which he obviously loves and finds very fulfilling. He works in his school all day long, teaching, and in the evening he goes home and works there on finding out designs for new types of instruments. He never seems to stop working, as he believes in what he is doing. He's very dedicated and committed to it. Sometimes he makes courses for special teachers and music teachers who want to teach with this method. I've been on a few of these courses, and one of the nicest things about them for me is that his excitement and enthusiasm for what he does are so strong as to be contagious. Everybody who goes there leaves filled up with inspiration and bubbling with ideas.

He now has three orchestras, which are really becoming quite famous and have made several cassettes of their music, and performed in many countries, including Portugal, Holland, Slovenia and Hungary. They are really very good, I think.

So after I discovered this method, I went to visit Dr. Ulrich in Germany to find out more about it, and then returned home to start to try to put this system into practice. Today we have a lot of groups, with ages ranging from young children to adults, and they all enjoy making music in this way immensely. We have two orchestras now, one made up of mentally handicapped blind people, who are really talented, and play a lot of concerts. They play not from colours and shapes, of course, but from a type of notation which is "written" using different textured materials, like wood, metal, and cloth. The other orchestra is made up of sighted mentally handicapped people, and they have recently performed three concerts with one of Dr Ulrich's German orchestras, which were very good and were a big experience and success for me too.

We have a lot of different types of instruments, such as a special type of pan-pipes which are put together piece by piece, so first the child is given a single flute of one pitch, and when he or she has learned to blow it another can be fitted on to the side of it, of a different pitch, and as he or she learns more of the symbols for the different pitches of notes, they get more and more different sized flutes to connect onto the end of the pan-pipes. We also have a variety of stringed instruments, some of which are solo instruments, for playing melodies, and some of which provide chords for accompaniment. We have xylophones made from metal, and a range of percussion instruments.

The tunes they play are from various types of music. They play children's songs, folk songs, easy excerpts from famous pieces of classical music and other things - with one of the orchestras we are presently learning a Negro spiritual.

I believe in this system of teaching very much, and hope very much that it will become more widely acknowledged and that its use will become more widespread. I plan to continue to work with it, because I find it very fulfilling. Yesterday I was ill, but not so badly ill that I couldn't make music with the children, so I went in anyway, as this work is very important to me.

Music Makes the World Go Round

1. What does Shannon do?
2. Why did she want to teach them to play music?
3. Why did everyone tell her it was impossible?
4. What did she find out?
5. What does Dr. Ulrich think of teaching these children to play music?
6. What does Dr. Ulrich propose about the difficulties?
7. What system has he created?
8. In what ways is his system different?
9. How many music lessons do the children have at his school?
10. What is the first lesson like?
11. What do they learn at the other lessons?

12. How can these lessons help the children develop?

13. What kind of person is Dr. Ulrich himself?

14. What is the best thing about his enthusiasm?

15. How many orchestras does he have now?

16. What does Shannon do to develop Dr. Ulrich's ideas?

17. How many orchestras do they have now?

18. Who are the orchestras made up of?

19. Who have they recently performed with?

20. What were the concerts like?

21. What is special about the pan-pipes they have?

22. What other instruments do they play?

23. What kind of tunes do they play?

24. What does Shannon hope for?

25. What shows her dedication to this work?

Music Makes the World Go Round

Training 1

Shannon works with mentally handicapped children. She has always observed how much they love music, and always wanted to find a way to teach them to play. All the books, however, and all the experts, told her that it was impossible until about ten years ago Dr. Ulrich began to teach the mentally handicapped children to play instruments. He says they should do it, as it's very good for them, and they enjoy it enormously.

Training 2

He has designed a great variety of instruments that the children can play, and proposes that the main problem has always been with the system of notation used to write music down. So he has created a special system which uses many different shapes and colours to represent the pitch and duration of the notes, instead of the usual mass of little black dots.

Training 3

Now he has a school, in Germany, where the children have three music lessons a day. The first lesson is a joyful session of singing and dancing, and the other two lessons are for teaching this special new system of reading music and learning to play the instruments. Children have a lot of success with it. Also, it is good for developing their physical co-ordination, counting, reading and concentration abilities.

Training 4

So after Shannon discovered this method, she went to visit Dr. Ulrich to find out more about it, and then returned home to start to put this system into practice. Today they have a lot of groups, and they all enjoy making music in this way immensely. They have two orchestras now, one made up of blind and the other made up of sighted mentally handicapped people.

Training 5

The tunes they play are from various types of music. They play children's songs, folk songs, easy excerpts from famous pieces of classical music and other things. And they have recently performed three concerts with one of Dr. Ulrich's German orchestras, which were very good and were a big experience and success for Shannon too.

A Real Globe-Trotter

My friend Mike is a road engineer. He was born in New Zealand, but lived for most of his life in Tasmania, as his parents emigrated there. His father is also an engineer of one sort or another, his mother is an accountant or something like that for a local company. He has two sisters and a brother, and he's the youngest one, I guess. His parents were born in England, and his sisters were born in Africa, when his parents were living somewhere in Kenya for a few years, but they ended up living in New Zealand and then Tasmania. One day he decided he wanted to travel through south-east Asia - he had a bit of money from working as a road engineer for four or five years after he finished college. He travelled extensively in Asia over a period of about two years, and could afford to do that as travel and the cost of living in Asia are generally really, really cheap. I don't know all the places he visited there - I know he spent time in India, in the Himalayas in the North, and by the sea on the south-west coast, and some time staying in Kathmandu in Nepal, where he recounted seeing many beautiful temples, including one full of monkeys, and meeting many warm, friendly Tibetan refugees. I think he also visited Thailand and Pakistan in that period.

Anyway, after that long excursion he flew to London to find all the relatives he had never met before, who he had only heard his parents speaking about. He met all his aunts and uncles, grannies and granddads, cousins and whatever, who lived all over England, and then went on to Norway, as he had some kind of family there as well. During the time he spent in Norway he worked in a fish factory shovelling frozen fish into containers, and made a fair amount of money doing it.

Then he went back to England and purchased a mobile home from a friend, a really nice one, about thirteen years old, with a diesel engine. The roof was elevated by an extendible plastic cover, so you could stand up inside it. He had a double bed in it, which folded up, and enough seats for six people in the back and three in the front, and it was all open, with no division between the driving and living sections. He had a small kitchen in the back, a small cupboard, and drawers with all kinds of exotic foods and spices in them, and running water coming from a tank which was built into the top. He had everything, and it was a really nice arrangement.

He also had a beautiful sound-system in it. Not that the tape recorder was of fantastic quality, but he had four speakers, two in the front and two in the back, which were purchased in a market where they take apart these video slot-machines, so they were heavy duty speakers. The friend who owned the van before him was a hi-fi maniac, so he knew all about the proper way to set up a system - he was into this "sound engineering" thing - so he attached paper tubes to the back or the speakers, and the whole thing, the length of the tubes, their distance from the walls of the van, the position of the speakers, all these things were precisely worked out to give the best possible sound.

His friend also left him a huge box of tapes to use during his trip, with a hundred and fifty or two hundred cassettes, really nice ones, and he had his old ones, a few, which he had brought from home. There were all kinds of music which I'd never heard before, folk music, a lot of "world music." Some of it sounded like it came from a different planet. Imagine a band where there's an African guy, an Irish guy, someone from South America maybe, and they all play instruments you've never heard of.

He had a few tapes of music featuring the didgeridoo, which is a traditional instrument of the Australian aborigines. You know, they don't have many instruments in their music, mostly just singing and the didgeridoo. The didgeridoo is a kind of tube, over a metre long, which is made from a branch of eucalyptus tree which has been hollowed out over the years by termites, little insects which eat the inside of the branch, living there for a while in large groups. And when they've eaten all they can, the tube is left completely hollow. The aboriginal people look for these in the outback, polish them up, paint sacred symbols on them, and then play them by vibrating their lips against one end of the tube. They make a kind of droning sound, sometimes making a rhythmic pulse, sometimes changing the shape of the mouth to make different noises, such as sounds to imitate those made by the animals and birds of the Australian outback. It's a really interesting sound, at times relaxing and hypnotising and at other times exciting and invigorating. Also, the sound is continuous. It doesn't have breaks in it. They achieve this by using a special kind of breathing, "circular breathing", which involves breathing out from the cheeks and into the lungs at the same time. It's really interesting!

Anyway, after getting his mobile home in England, he just drove around Europe, visiting friends in different countries and visiting sights of natural interest all over Europe, as he loves nature and seems to have a great desire to see as many places and things as he possibly can. Altogether, he was travelling around for about four years, being a real globe-trotter. Now he's returned to his parents' place in Tasmania to finish building a house there that he started a while before he left. I just got a letter from him saying that when he finishes that, he wants to go and visit his sisters, who now live in Queensland in north-east Australia, and work there for a while, probably as a road engineer, then hit the road again for another few years.

A Real Globe-Trotter

1. What is Mike?

2. Where was he born?

3. Where did he live for most of his life?

4. Where were his parents born?

5. Where were his sisters born?

6. Where did he decide to travel first?

7. How long did he travel around Asia?

8. How could he afford such a long journey?

9. Which places and countries did he visit?

10. Where did he fly after that?

11. Who did he want to meet there?

12. How did he happen to go to Norway as well?

13. What did he do while he was living in Norway?

14. What did he buy when he came back to England?

15. What was special about the roof of the van?

16. What furniture and facilities did the van have?

17. What was special about the sound-system he had in the van?

18. Who set up the sound system?

19. What kind of music did that friend leave him?

20. What is a didgeridoo?

21. What is it made from?

22. What kind of sound does this instrument produce?

23. What did Mike do after getting the mobile home?

24. Why has he returned to Tasmania?

25. What is he going to do after he finishes the house?

A Real Globe-Trotter

Training 1

My friend Mike is a road engineer. He was born in New Zealand, but lived for most of his life in Tasmania. He has two sisters and a brother. His parents were born in England, and his sisters were born in Africa, when his parents were living somewhere in Kenya for a few years, but they ended up living in New Zealand and then Tasmania.

Training 2

One day he decided to travel through south-east Asia. He had a bit of money from working as a road engineer for four or five years. So he travelled extensively in Asia over a period of about two years. He spent time in India, in the Himalayas, by the sea , and in Kathmandu in Nepal, where he saw many beautiful temples, including one full of monkeys, and met many friendly Tibetan refugees. He also visited Thailand and Pakistan in that period.

Training 3

After that long excursion he flew to London to find all the relatives he had never met before. He met all his aunts and uncles, grannies and granddads, cousins and whatever, who lived all over England, and then went on to Norway, as he had some kind of family there as well. During the time he spent in Norway he worked in a fish factory shovelling frozen fish into containers, and made a fair amount of money doing it.

Training 4

Then he went back to England and purchased a mobile home from a friend, with a diesel engine. He had a double bed in it, and enough seats for six people in the back and three in the front. He had a small kitchen in the back, and running water coming from a tank which was built into the top. He had everything, and it was a really nice arrangement.

Training 5

Then he just drove around Europe, visiting friends and sights of natural interest all over Europe. Altogether, he was travelling around for about four years, being a real globe-trotter. Now he's returned to his parents' place in Tasmania to finish building a house. When he finishes that, he wants to go and visit his sisters, who now live in Australia, and work there for a while, then hit the road again for another few years.

Neighbours

My girlfriend and I live in a cosy little flat in the eleventh district of Budapest, with one big living room, which we sleep in, a tiny little kitchen, a bathroom and a hallway. It's quite a small place, but that's okay, especially in the winter, as winters here are very long and it's easy to heat. It's one of these post-war apartment buildings with about thirty apartments, at a rough guess. So we have plenty of neighbours, although I do believe that we're the only people below thirty years old that live in the entire building. Our neighbours are all quite old, and mostly sort of kind, but some of them get quite angry. We don't talk to them very often, except when we're responding to their threats, or when they're yelling at us for one reason or another.

Some of them can be pretty offensive - in fact, they managed to drive out our last next-door neighbours, who were also a younger group of people, I think aged about thirty. The rest of the tenants are apartment owners, whereas we just rent our flat. Anyway, the people living next door to us belonged to a Christian group. I'm not sure what denomination they were, but they were really into singing Christian songs. I think that they belonged to a choir, or something like that. They decided that they would record their songs in the apartment, I think. It seemed that the place was being used as a studio. There were many people coming and going at various hours of the day, and the other neighbours weren't too happy about this, especially the woman below them, who is, in fact, mad. She's completely insane.

In order to enter the building, you need to ring the buzzer, which makes an annoying high-pitched droning noise, before you can be let in by the person you're visiting. Now, there's a note on the door saying not to slam it shut, but, of course, most of the people who come to visit us can't read Hungarian, so they don't understand what it says and they let the door slam shut. That, understandably, really annoys the woman who lives right next door to the entrance. She acts as a kind of gatekeeper for the whole building. She's quite old, but she can sometimes muster up enough energy to really scare the wits out of people. You could ask anyone who's come to visit us and has been confronted by her!

She's a sweet old lady really, though. She's not to be confused, however, with the insane woman who lives on the second floor, underneath our old neighbours' flat next to us on the third floor, which is now empty. Like I said before, she's mad. She screams at anyone who enters the building, attempting to find out who they are, what they're doing, who they're going to visit, and, in fact, she even demanded some of our friends tell her why they were in the country! I think she's the house xenophobe, and she's proved her aggressiveness on several occasions, one of them being when she had it out with the Christian choir living next door to us. She had a shouting battle with them from the second floor up to the third floor, in fact, maybe they met halfway, I'm not sure, to exchange words. She told them that they shouldn't have guests coming into the building all the time, and that the house is not a barn for people to be running in and out of all the time. I think she was trying to assert the authority of her age, I'm not sure, but anyway, she still lives there and the people next door don't any more. I hope we're not next!

Sometimes, on occasion, she teams up with the woman who lives directly below us, whose name is Mrs. K. . She's a really short little old lady who likes to walk around in her dressing-gown, and she frequently comes up to visit us, because our bathroom floor leaks through to her bathroom ceiling. Actually, I think the leak is coming from a pipe somewhere between our floor and her ceiling, as she often has a wet ceiling even when we haven't had a wet floor. So, she comes up and visits us from time to time. Sometimes she's wearing her teeth and sometimes she's not, which can make it more or less easy to understand her - my Hungarian isn't fantastic at the best of times. She has very short, thinly- spread hair. When she goes out shopping she puts in her teeth and wears a smudge of sort of mauve-coloured lipstick, but when she wants to come and complain to us, she usually forgets her teeth and just wears a nightgown. As I said, she sometimes teams up with the other lady on the premise of complaining about something, usually.

Actually, I think Mrs. K. is a little mad also. Pretty crazy. She used to only visit us when she wanted to complain about the drip coming from her ceiling, but of late she's become less belligerent. The other day she woke us up at seven thirty in the morning, catching us a little off our guard, to show us a letter which had been returned to her from the US. She'd addressed this letter to "Paramount Pictures, Hollywood, California." It took some deciphering to even read that much, as the writing was a blurred scrawl - if I could show it to you you'd understand - and she didn't know the exact address. I think she just hoped it'd get there. It came back with a notice stamped on it saying, "Return to sender", in English, so it had obviously reached the States but the address had been insufficient. She came up to us claiming that since I was American I should know what this was all about, that as an American I was in some way responsible for it, and that I should somehow rectify the issue. We accepted her request and said we'd look into it. She wanted us to look at the letter right there, so we had a look at it, and she explained that there's an actor called Richard Dean Anderson, who plays a television character called MacGyver, who I wasn't familiar with. The letter was supposed to somehow get to him, as she explained that she's in love with him, and she wanted a picture of him. She had a small picture that she had cut out of some TV magazine, which she had enclosed in the envelope, but she wanted a big picture of him. All of this came out in a burbling stream of Hungarian, which I don't really understand very well in the first place, but luckily my girlfriend Vera was there to help me. So we finally understood what the problem was, and told her we'd try to find out what the real address was and send it on, and rewrite the letter. You see, the whole thing was actually written in Hungarian, so she had assumed somehow that the people who were going to read this letter would understand Hungarian, and promptly get a picture and send it to her.

So, we immediately saw that this wouldn't work, and that we'd have to translate the letter into English for her, which we immediately said we'd do as she was getting quite excited at that point. We did that, and somehow found an address which we could send the letter to.

The letter went something like this:

"To whom it may concern,

I'm kindly requesting that you send me a photo of Richard Dean Anderson, the actor who plays MacGyver, and would like you to inform him that he's very welcome to visit me.

Thanking you kindly in advance, Mrs. K. "

Neighbours

1. Where do Paul and Vera live?
2. Why don't they care that their flat is quite small?
3. What kind of building do they live in?
4. How many neighbours do they have?
5. How old are all of them?
6. What are they like?
7. When can't Paul and Vera help talking to them?
8. What happened to Paul and Vera's last next-door neighbours?
9. What were those neighbours fond of?
10. What did they want to do in the apartment?
11. What was the problem with the apartment being used as a studio?
12. What do you have to do to enter the building?
13. Why are frequent visitors so annoying for the neighbours?
14. Why do some of Paul's guests let the door slam shut?
15. What can the old lady living next to the entrance do to careless guests?

16. Why is she not to be confused with the one who lives on the 2nd floor?

17. How does the latter react to anyone who enters the building?

18. What did she demand some of their friends do?

19. How did she manage to drive their next-door neighbours out?

20. Who does she sometimes team up with?

21. Why do they often have to meet the woman who lives below them?

22. What does she look like?

23. What does Paul think of her?

24. Why and what time did she bring the letter to Hollywood to them?

25. What was peculiar about that letter?

Neighbours

Training 1

Paul and Vera live in a little flat in the eleventh district of Budapest. It's one of post-war apartment buildings with about thirty apartments. So they have plenty of neighbours. Their neighbours are all quite old, and some of them get quite angry. They don't talk to them very often, except when they're responding to their threats, or when they're yelling at Paul and Vera.

Training 2

In fact, they managed to drive out Paul's last next-door neighbours who belonged to a Christian group and were into singing songs. They wanted to record them in the apartment. And the other neighbours weren't too happy about this, especially the woman below them. She had a shouting battle with them and told them that they shouldn't have guests coming into the building all the time. She still lives there but they don't any more.

Training 3

In order to enter the building, you need to ring the buzzer, which makes an annoying high-pitched noise. Also, there's a note on the door saying not to slam it shut, but most of Paul's visitors can't read Hungarian, so they let the door slam shut. That, understandably, really annoys the woman who lives right next door to the entrance. She's quite old, but she can sometimes muster up enough energy to really scare the wits out of people!

Training 4

There is also Mrs. K. who lives directly below Paul. She's a really short little old lady who likes to walk around in her dressing-gown, and she frequently comes up to visit them, because their bathroom floor leaks through to her bathroom ceiling. Sometimes she's wearing her teeth and sometimes she's not, which can make it difficult to understand her.

Training 5

Once she woke them up at seven thirty in the morning to show them a letter which had been returned to her from the US. She claimed that since Paul was American he should know what this was all about. The letter was supposed to get to some actor in Hollywood, as she wanted a picture of him. So they told her they'd find out what the real address was and rewrite the letter as the whole thing was actually written in Hungarian!

Travels with My Saxophone

I was travelling, on my way to Dublin in a sort of roundabout way, coming from the south of England up to Scotland, and I was planning to go up around Scotland for a while, across the Irish sea to Northern Ireland, and then down south to Dublin. However, I got stopped in my tracks in Glasgow by catching glandular fever, a viral disease which attacks your lungs and your throat and takes all the energy out of your body, so I had to stay there to recuperate. Having nowhere to go when I came out of the hospital, I went into a homeless hostel, which was quite a rough place, as most of the people there had come there from prison, so it wasn't very nice really. I didn't have any money, so I started busking with my newly acquired saxophone.

It was around Christmas time, so I played a lot of Christmas carols and improvised variations on their tunes. So I'd go out busking every day of the week, every day of the month, for what seemed like a really long time, and that's how I learned to play the saxophone. I got very friendly with a lot of people from there, especially with a lot of the other buskers - there was a sort of busker culture where everybody knew everybody else. Most people were not spoken of by their names - I was, for instance, "The little Irish man who plays the saxophone." There was "Billy Hendrix", a small guy who had a little amplifier powered by batteries and an electric guitar, who used to play Jimmy Hendrix songs all night, and who used to make a lot of money doing that. There was another saxophone player who looked like someone out of "The Muppets", a children's TV programme where we come from featuring a lot of young puppets who just run around having a good time. He really looked like a muppet.

Then there was "Billy with the Loud Voice", who used to sing slow rock songs in his own inimitable fashion, singing very loudly. You could hear him from miles away. He let me know of a place for rent on the west side of Glasgow. It was a house full of bedsits, one of which he occupied - a bedsit being a room with a bed and a cooker in it. If you were unemployed you could apply for housing benefit, and there was a particularly understanding landlord who, if you gave him one month's rent in advance, and one hundred pounds as a deposit, would let you a room.

So, I decided I was going to try to get this bedsit, and I worked very hard, busking all day, trying to make as much money as I could, and the day came when I almost had enough money to get this place to stay. I was a hundred pounds short, and I thought I wasn't going to get it. How could I earn a hundred pounds by the next day? So I resigned myself to the fact that I was going to have to stay in the hostel for a while longer. Anyway, I got a phone call from my friend Eddie, Eddie O'Neill, and he said, "Would you like to come up to Alec's house, and we'll play some music together?" Alec and Eddie were two guitarists that I used to busk with regularly, and we used to play songs by The Waterboys, Van Morrison, and such things. So I said, "Yes, of course. I'll meet you there." He said, "You don't need to, my brother is here, and he has a car, so we'll come and pick you up." I sat on the fourth floor of the hostel, looking out of the window, waiting for the car. The car arrived, and my friend Eddie got out and waved to me, so I picked up my saxophone and ran downstairs, went out of the front door, and got into the car. Now Alec lived about two and a half miles away. In the car, Eddie was asking me, "So, how are you getting on trying to get the money for a proper place to stay?" I said, "I'm a hundred pounds short, and tomorrow is the deadline, so I can't get it." He said, "Oh, that's a shame", and we talked for a while on the way up the road.

When we arrived at Alec's house, I said to Eddie's brother, who had been sitting in the front of the car, "Thanks a lot for the lift." He turned round and handed me a hundred pounds, and said, "Pay me back when you can"! So I smiled gleefully, and didn't know what to say. "Thank you" didn't seem enough. I was speechless.

I had the money so I got the flat, and shortly after that, a few days later, I was busking again on the streets, and I didn't have a bad day, so I decided to go for a drink, because the band of a friend of mine were playing in this pub. I went along, and went down the stairs, and Stevie, the singer of the band, said, "Kenny!" "Hello

Stevie", I said. "Did you bring your saxophone?", he said. "Yes", I said. "Oh good", he replied, "because Bob, our saxophone player, has gone away to Manchester to visit his daughter for her birthday. So, will you play with us?" Of course I said yes. So I played the gig. I wasn't particularly good, but I was okay, and after the concert they paid me twenty-five pounds, which was a vast amount of money for me at the time. I needed to start saving to pay back my hundred pound debt, so I was very, very pleased.

Then one of the people in the band said "Do you see that man over there? He's the singer, and the leader, of a band whose saxophone player has just left", so I, feeling very confident after my first paid gig, went over to him and said, "I hear that your band no longer has a saxophone player. Would you like one?" "Well, yes", he said, "but I'm really looking for someone who plays more than just saxophone, someone that plays the flute and maybe the Irish whistle as well." I quickly replied, "Yes, that's me, I play all of those!", which was a slight exaggeration as I'd never played the flute before in my life, but I thought I could learn fast enough. He said, "Okay, what are you doing in two weeks' time?" I said, "Nothing", and he asked, "Would you like to go to Germany on tour, with my band." I said, "Of course, I'd love to", and so it was there and then decided that I would tour Germany, with a band I'd never even heard before, in two weeks. In that time, I had to somehow get hold of a flute and learn how to play it. Luckily, I was soon able to borrow a flute, and I played it very hard for two weeks and then went on tour with the band, not knowing any of the songs, or anything at all about the band, really.

I spent six weeks in Germany touring with them, and over the next nine months I went to Germany four times with them, having a very good time, staying in hotels and being fully fed and watered. My first gig with them was my second paid concert ever, and I was on a European tour with a rock band!

There was a place that we played every month that we were there, on each tour that we did, and the third time that we went there was in the festival season, which is in November in the east of Germany. During this time we played sometimes three concerts a day, often two hundred kilometres apart, so we were very busy.

And we went to play at this place, in Jena, and the man who was organizing it had arranged a football match for us, and gathered up all of the English speaking people around to make a team, with spaces for myself and the others in the band. So, we played this game of football against the German team, and were thoroughly beaten, but it was very good fun. After this we went and had a shower, and went on to the concert. By this time we were very tired, as we'd already performed in another place that morning, and we'd finished the night before at six o'clock.

So we just kept on going, and went on to do the concert. Now, traditionally, one "set" of songs is forty-five minutes long, and the contract says that you have to do two sets, so you play for forty-five minutes, then have a break, and then play for another forty-five minutes. This we did, but after the second forty-five minutes the clientele of the establishment were having a very good time, and the boss requested that we play again, for another forty-five minutes. Now this was a lot to ask for, as we were very tired, so we said no. Well, the boss said, "If I give you another hundred marks, would you consider it?" and we said, "Okay, just for you", and we did another forty-five minute set, after which he said, "Will you play another forty-five minute set?", to which we again replied, "No." He again said, "What if I give you another hundred marks?", to which we again replied, "Yes." So we did yet another set, by which time it was getting rather late, or should I say early in the morning. But nobody seemed to mind, and the boss asked us to play again. We said no again, and the boss said, "I'll give you another hundred marks" again, but this time we were so burned out that we flatly said no. It could have gone on for the rest of the next day. So we finished the concert and went outside for some air, as it was very hot in there, under the lights, very hot and sweaty, and we sat down and relaxed and had a beer, but the place was still packed full of people - it was about five o' clock by this time. After a couple of beers, we went back into the pub, and as soon as we opened the door, the crowd erupted very noisily, shouting and clapping at us, patting us all on the back, to get us back on stage. However, the singer was not in the mood for this.

What eventually happened was that I walked up to the stage on my own, picked up my saxophone, sat down on the edge of the stage, and started to play, very slowly, not playing any particular tune but just improvising, making things up. I played for about half an hour, and then ended on one very long note. As I finished there was silence. I had had my eyes closed all of the time, and I realized that there was silence, and I thought that maybe everyone had left. So I opened my eyes, and the place was still cram packed full of people, hundreds of them, and they were all just listening to me. Then they all went mad again screaming and shouting, and buying me beers. It was just amazing. It was one of the most amazing feelings I've ever had in my entire life.

Travels with My Saxophone

1. Where was Mike travelling?
2. Why did he get stopped in Glasgow?
3. Where did he go when he came out of the hospital?
4. What kind of place was that hostel?
5. What did Mike start doing to earn his living?
6. What kind of tunes did he play?
7. How did he learn to play the saxophone?
8. Who did he make friends with?
9. What was interesting about the buskers' names?
10. Who told him of a place for rent?
11. What is a typical bedsit like?
12. What did you have to do to get a bedsit?
13. What did he have to do to save enough money to rent a place to stay?
14. How much was he short the day before the deadline?
15. Who lent him a necessary hundred pounds?

16. How did Mike feel when his friend's brother handed him the money?

17. Where did he go for a drink a few days later?

18. What did the singer of the band suggest Mike did?

19. How much did he get for his first paid gig?

20. Who was the leader of another band looking for?

21. What did he offer Mike to do?

22. How much time did Mike have to learn to play the flute?

23. How long did they tour Germany?

24. What was extraordinary about Mike participating?

25. What did he feel after he had been playing alone?

Travels with My Saxophone

Training 1

Mike was travelling, on his way to Dublin in a sort of roundabout way. However, he got stopped in Glasgow by catching glandular fever, so he had to stay there to recuperate. When he came out of the hospital, he went into a homeless hostel, which was quite a rough place. He didn't have any money, so he started busking with his newly acquired saxophone.

Training 2

So he'd go out busking every day of the week, and that's how he learned to play the saxophone. Mike got very friendly with a lot of other buskers. And one of them let him know of a place for rent. It was a house full of bedsits. And if you gave the landlord one month's rent in advance, and one hundred pounds as a deposit, he would let you a room.

Training 3

So, he decided to get this bedsit. But he still was a hundred pounds short. And then suddenly one of his new friends lent him a hundred pounds! So he got the flat. A few days later, he was asked to play with some band because their saxophone player had gone away to visit his daughter. So Mike played the gig. And after the concert they paid him twenty-five pounds. He needed to start saving to pay back his debt, so he was very, very pleased.

Training 4

Then he met the leader of a band - he was looking for someone that played the saxophone, the flute and the Irish whistle as well. Mike quickly replied that he played all of those, even though he'd never played the flute before. And so he was going to tour Germany, with a band he'd never even heard before, in two weeks. In that time, he had to learn how to play the flute. And he played it very hard for two weeks and then went on tour.

Training 5

He spent six weeks in Germany touring with them, and over the next nine months he went to Germany four times, having a very good time and being fully fed and watered. And though his first gig with them was his second paid concert ever, he was on a European tour with a rock band! He even played alone in the place cram packed full of people and they were all listening to him. It was one of the most amazing feelings he'd ever had.

Camping Nightmares

I'm the kind of person who always leaves things until the last minute. I never prepare for things weeks in advance, and usually get ready for holidays and excursions just before I have to leave. I was embarking on a trip over the Irish Sea, to visit Ireland, and I knew that it would probably rain, as all my friends who had been there had told me that it never stops raining there. Actually, I found out that it wasn't so bad, as although it rains five times a day, it only seems to come in short bursts. It generally rained for maybe twenty minutes and then stopped, which was comfortable enough for me, as when I returned to my home in the north of England it was much colder and rained for five hours a day. So, of course, I needed a tent, but as usual I waited for three hours before my train left before going out to buy a tent. I went to a department store very close to my home, and for twenty-nine pounds and ninety-nine pence I bought a very cheap but, I thought, very nice tent. I thought that, as I didn't have so much money, I might find myself in the situation that I was out walking or hitch-hiking, and it could start to rain, and I would need something to put over my things to keep them dry, something that would also not be too heavy to carry, so I looked around in the store and found a nice large plastic tarpaulin which folded up into a small light bundle, and bought that. It was very cheap, a couple of pounds as I remember, but it folded out to a huge size - it was eighteen square metres when fully open.

During my trip I visited Galway, and one night there I had put up my tent in a field and gone to the nearest small town to look for a cosy pub to sit in, preferably with some music happening in it. It rained a little while I was in the pub, and I sat talking to some locals, but overall it was a fairly uneventful evening. Afterwards I went back to the tent, not knowing if it would be soaked through with water, but I was very happy to find that it was quite dry inside. I got undressed and climbed into my sleeping bag, and tried to sleep. It was very windy, and I lay awake for a while listening to the wind, and I had just managed to fall asleep when I was awoken by a very cold drop of water on my face. I tried to carry on sleeping, but again and again I was dripped on, until I found that I was really starting to get quite wet. What was happening was that the pressure of the wind was forcing the raindrops through the lining of the tent, so I took out my plastic sheet and put it over the top of me and all of my things, inside the tent. I tried to sleep again, and nearly managed, but I was thinking so hard about the plastic over my head, that maybe it wouldn't let any air through and I would suffocate. So I uncovered my head, and then again, sploosh, I was being dripped on. I didn't sleep much that night. When I woke up in the morning, the plastic sheet was covered with small puddles of rainwater. The next night the weather was the same, with some wind and rain, so I thought to be a bit cleverer I might cover the whole tent with the plastic. So I fixed the plastic sheet over the tent, with some rocks, and went into the tent. All of my clothes, my sleeping bag, and all of my thing were dry by that time, as the day had been sunny and I had put them all out in the sun, so I went to bed thinking my troubles with the weather were over.

But halfway through the night, while I was sleeping, I awoke suddenly as half of the tent was falling on top of me. So I got out of the tent, in the pouring rain, and tried to reassemble it, then crawled back into my sleeping bag, wet to the bone from being outside in the rain. I nearly got back to sleep, when, guess what, I started to feel cold wet drops of water falling on my face, like on the previous night. So I went out again, and saw that this time the wind had blown the plastic sheet completely off of the tent, and it was slowly being blown across the field. I retrieved it, and set it up again, but by that time everything had started to get drenched again and I had an altogether miserable, cold, wet night.

Two years later I returned to Ireland, but this time I thought that it would be more intelligent not to go with a thirty pound tent but to invest a bit in a better one which would stay up and keep me dry. I looked around, and, acting on the advice of a friend, went to a camping store and bought a much better one. It was not so small, and had a much thicker, waterproof lining.

One day I decided to go to visit a friend that I had met when I was there before. She didn't have a telephone at home, but had given me the telephone number of her workplace. So, at this time I was in the north, and I decided to hitchhike to where she lived, in County Kerry. I thought that it would take two days, that I would arrive two days later, but the hitchhiking was much more successful that I imagined it would be, and I got there very quickly. I stayed one night in Killarney, and the next day started again for Kerry. I knew that she would leave work at about five o'clock, and as it was about four I thought I should go to the nearest village to find a telephone. But a car stopped and the driver asked, "Where do you want to go?" and I told him, and he replied that he could take me a very long way in the direction of my destination. I thanked him very much, and told him that there was a problem, that I needed to telephone before five o'clock. He said, "No problem, no problem. Here you are", and handed me a mobile telephone, and I had never seen one before so I was a little nervous handling it. I didn't really know how to use it, so I asked, "Where do I have to press?" and he said, "Give it to me. I'll do it for you." He pressed a couple of buttons, and I took the telephone back and dialed the number, and heard a very very faint voice coming from the telephone. I couldn't understand what it was saying, so I just asked if I could speak to my friend. There was no sound, and then one minute later another voice came. I said my name, and I heard some kind of "Ah!" in response, so I knew I was talking to the right person, and she said something else which I couldn't understand. I said, "I can't hear anything, could you please talk louder?" and she responded again but I couldn't understand a word, and by this time I was getting a bit frustrated. I said to the driver, "Is it possible to close the window?", and he closed the window but I still couldn't really hear what she was saying. I asked if it was possible to make the volume louder, and the driver said, "You have to press here", so I did, and the sound disappeared completely. I was horrified.

I dialed again, and heard her voice again, but still sounding very faint and distant. The driver said, "Give it to me", and then took it, turned it round and then handed it back to me. I felt so embarrassed. I had been holding the telephone upside-down all of the time. So now, of course, I could hear her voice crystal clear.

Well, it was too late to meet her that evening, as she said that she already had an appointment with somebody, so I decided to visit another friend who lived nearby, in Killarney, which was in the direction we were headed in. So I looked for the telephone number in my book, found it, and rang again from the car. A woman answered who was very friendly, and told me that my friend, Nicola, was not there, but if I tried to call back later I might catch her in. Well, I called again later, and she still wasn't in, but the lady said, "Come anyway, she'll surely be back later on" and gave me directions.

We arrived in Killarney and I asked the driver to drop me off, then I had a stiff walk uphill with all of my baggage. I was shocked, because the area I was heading into, which I had directions to go to, was such a rich area, with one deluxe villa next to another. I didn't perceive my friend to be so well off, so I thought : "I must be in the wrong place." But no, the directions seemed to fit. I asked the way three or four times until I found myself at the grandest, most impressive, biggest luxury villa in the neighbourhood, and this was the place that I had directions for. I was so shy that on seeing the people in the doorway, who looked very rich, I went into a nearby forest to hide my rucksack and other baggage before I dared to approach the house.

I knocked, and a very friendly woman answered the door, and invited me to come inside and wait. I went to get my things and sat down inside, and she fed me a very tasty dinner, and then Nicola's brother came back, and said that Nicola wouldn't be back that night, but he knew where she was, and although he couldn't take me there he could arrange for his friend to later on. But first, he said, I should put up my tent in the garden, in a field next to the house where some horses were grazing. I joked that when I woke up a horse would be lying beside me, and he convinced me: "Don't be afraid. They won't do anything to you. You'll be perfectly okay. "

I set up my tent and then left with Nicola's brother's friend. We got into town and went straight to the pub where Nicola usually went, and we didn't find her there but decided to stay there for the evening, as we had no other ideas as to where she might be, and there was a really good session happening in the pub. I had my guitar, and asked if I could play with them, and they replied, "Of course, of course, come and sit down. " Well, there were no seats free, but Irish people are really friendly, and one man who wasn't playing gave me his chair so that I could sit down and play. I had a thoroughly enjoyable evening there, playing until about two in the morning, with very very good musicians. One of the accordion players said that he had won the All-Ireland championship a couple of years before, being awarded the prize for Best Accordion Player.

When I returned to the house I found that the tent had completely collapsed, and was flat on the floor, as the horses had sat on it while I was in the town. I crawled into the smashed up tent and tried to sleep, but I was really afraid that a horse would come and trample all over me, or sit on me, in the night, so I went off to sleep in a barn. I was infuriated!

Camping Nightmares

1. What is Joshua like?

2. Where was he going?

3. Why did he need a tent?

4. Why didn't he mind the rain in Ireland?

5. Why did he have to buy a tent in the nearest department store?

6. What else did he buy there?

7. Where did he put up his tent in Galway?

8. Where did he spend the evening?

9. What was the weather like?

10. Did he find his tent dry inside?

11. What was he awoken by?

12. What was happening?

13. What did he do to protect himself and his things?

14. What was he afraid of?

15. What happened as soon as he uncovered his head?

16. What did he do the next night to prevent the same trouble?

17. Why did he awake halfway through the night?

18. What happened after he had reassembled the tent?

19. Why couldn't he sleep even after he had retrieved the plastic sheet?

20. What kind of tent did he buy for his next visit to Ireland?

21. Who did decide to visit?

22. Why wasn't his friend in when he arrived?

23. Where did he have to set up the tent?

24. What did he discover when he returned from the pub?

25. Why did he end up sleeping in a barn?

Camping Nightmares

Training 1

Joshua's the kind of person who always leaves things until the last minute. He was going to visit Ireland and knew that it would probably rain. So he needed a tent, but as usual he waited for three hours before his train left. So he went to a department store and bought a very cheap tent. He also found a large plastic tarpaulin and bought that.

Training 2

One rainy night was very windy, and he had just managed to fall asleep when he was awoken by a very cold drop of water on his face. The pressure of the wind was forcing the raindrops through the lining of the tent, so he took out a plastic sheet and put it over the top of him. He tried to sleep again, but he was afraid, that he'd suffocate. So he uncovered his head, and then again he was being dripped on. He didn't sleep much that night.

Training 3

The next night he fixed the plastic sheet over the tent. But halfway through the night, he awoke suddenly as half of the tent was falling on him. So he got out of the tent, in the pouring rain, and tried to reassemble it. He nearly got back to sleep, when he started to feel cold drops of water falling on his face because the wind had blown the plastic sheet off of the tent. Joshua set it up again, but he had an altogether miserable, cold, wet night.

Training 4

Two years later he returned to Ireland, but this time he bought a much better tent. One day he decided to hitchhike to see his friend Nicola. The driver lent him a mobile phone to let her know he was coming but he could hardly hear anything. When he arrived Nicola wasn't in, but her brother told him where she was. He also told him to put up his tent in a field where some horses were grazing.

Training 5

Joshua set up his tent and then went to the pub where Nicola usually went. He didn't find her but he had an enjoyable evening there. When he returned, he found that the tent had completely collapsed, as the horses had sat on it. He crawled into it and tried to sleep, but he was afraid that a horse would sit on him, so he went off to sleep in a barn. He was infuriated!

The Secret Tunnel

There is a really beautiful old church in our parish, in the middle of our village, which dates back to the early Middle Ages. This church was rebuilt several times, but parts of the church, including the foundations, are original. A while ago, some money was raised to install a heating system in the church, as it's quite big and it really needed one as it sometimes gets really cold, especially in the winter time. So, the money was collected, and the gas people came to work there. The vicar asked for some help, because some of the pipes of the new heating system were to go underneath the floor and there are many heavy benches in the church, which needed to be removed during the operation. Some of the local boys volunteered to help, and I was one of them. The benches were connected together in stacks, and so it was hard work to lift or to push them away, but we managed it.

Most of the church floor was covered with a kind of marble slabs, the same as you can find in many other churches, but under where the benches were, there was an area where there was no marble, but some ancient-looking bricks. We were really excited to think of what it could be, as we had heard stories about there being an old underground passageway, leading from a crypt beneath the area of the church, and that this passageway had been connected with the castle in the nearest city, twelve miles away, since mediaeval times.

So, a friend of mine and I started to try to dig down there. It was relatively easy to pull out the top layer of bricks, and underneath them we found soil. It was easy to dig the soil, as it was completely dry, having been closed off underneath the church for such a long time, and you could just sweep it out. I had to leave for a few minutes, as I had to sort out some papers in a nearby office, but my friend continued digging. So I left, and was quick to return, as I was so excited. It didn't take ten minutes. I came back, and rushed into the church, and I saw my friend standing in a hole up to his shoulders, with a big pile of earth next to him beside the hole. It was quite amazing to see him there like that, after seeing the church so many times before, every Sunday, and not thinking twice about the floor, and realize that a very short distance beneath the floor we usually stand on is soil. My friend was pulling out some bones, real human bones, and making a pile of them on the floor! There seemed to be many sets of bones down there, skeletons of many people. We found that one side of the hole was so soft that you could just push a stick through it, with no resistance, just push it through. It was obviously a passageway, it lead somewhere, for sure. We were so excited, you know. We had found the passageway, and we had found the crypt, everything, you know, and you know I really love mediaeval stuff.

Then some workmen came in, and they told us to stop, because we should call an archaeologist to take the things out correctly, as this could be a real historical find, and a doctor because the bones could be infected with some disease from the Middle Ages and cause a big epidemic. They told us to put all of the earth back, and then the vicar came and said, "Oh, don't bother with it, it's just too much of a headache. " So we were there, you know, in the heat of this discovery, and we had to just put all of the bones and soil back in the ground again.

We were so angry! After a few days, the workmen put a layer of hard cement over the entire floor, so this remained our mystery. I'm sure we found the passageway, but I don't know when the next time will be that someone bothers to see what's underneath the church. That was such a good time to excavate it, as they couldn't use the church anyway because of the work being done there, and the benches were all out of the way. Now that the benches are all back and the floor coated with cement, who's going to see what's there?

The Secret Tunnel

1. What is church in Mike's parish like?
2. Are there any original parts from the Middle Ages?
3. Why did the church need a heating system?
4. Where did the money for its installation come from?

5. Why did the vicar ask the boys to help?

6. What did they have to do?

7. What was the floor under the benches covered with?

8. Why were the boys so excited to discover that difference?

9. Who started to dig down there?

10. Was it hard work?

11. Why was it so easy to dig the soil?

12. Why did Mike have to leave for a while?

13. How long was he out?

14. What did he see when he returned?

15. What was it amazing to see such a deep hole in the church?

16. What was his friend pulling out?

17. What was unusual about one side of the hole?

18. What must it have been?

19. Why were the boys so exhilarated?

20. What did the workmen tell them to do?

21. What should they call an archaeologist for?

22. Why was the doctor to be called, too?

23. What was the vicar's reaction?

24. Why were the boys angry?

25. What happened a few days later?

The Secret Tunnel

Training 1

There is a really beautiful old church in Mike's parish, which dates back to the early Middle Ages. A while ago, some money was raised to install a heating system in the church, and the gas people came to work there. The vicar asked for some help, because there are many heavy benches in the church, which needed to be removed during the operation. Some of the local boys volunteered to help, and Mike was one of them.

Training 2

Most of the church floor was covered with a kind of marble slabs, but under the benches there was an area where there were some ancient-looking bricks. The boys were really excited about it, as they had heard stories about an old underground passageway, leading from a crypt beneath the area of the church, and connected with the castle in the nearest city.

Training 3

So, Mike and his friend started to dig down there. It was relatively easy to pull out the top layer of bricks, and underneath them they found soil. It was easy to dig the soil. Mike had to leave for a few minutes, and when he came back, his friend was pulling out real human bones, and making a pile of them on the floor! They found that one side of the hole was so soft that you could just push a stick through it. It was obviously a passageway.

Training 4

They were so excited. They had found the passageway, and they had found the crypt. Then some workmen came in, and they told them to stop, because they should call an archaeologist to take the things out correctly, and a doctor because the bones could be infected with some disease. They told them to put all of the earth back, and then the vicar came and told them not to bother as it was just too much of a headache.

Training 5

So they were in the heat of this discovery, and they had just to put all of the bones and soil back in the ground again. They were so angry! After a few days, the workmen put a layer of hard cement over the entire floor, so this remained their mystery. Mike is sure nobody is going to see what's there now that the benches are all back and the floor is coated with cement.

Printed in Great Britain
by Amazon